AN APOLOGY

FOR

MOHAMMED AND THE KORAN.

BY

JOHN DAVENPORT,

AUTHOR OF THE 'LIFE OF ALI PACHA OF JANINA;' 'OUDE VINDICATED;' 'KOORG
AND ITS RAJAHS;' 'AIDE MEMOIRE TO THE HISTORY OF INDIA;' 'HISTORICAL
CLASS BOOK,' AND VARIOUS EDUCATIONAL WORKS.

Contents:

I. MOHAMMED: A BIOGRAPHY.
II. THE KORAN AND ITS MORALITY.
III. CHARGES AGAINST MOHAMMED REFUTED.
IV. BEAUTIES OF THE KORAN.

"I confess I can make nothing of the critics in these times, who would accuse Mohammed of deceit *prepense;* of conscious deceit generally, or, perhaps, at all; still more, of living in a mere element of conscious deceit, and writing this Koran as a forger and a juggler would have done. Every candid eye, I think, will read the Koran far otherwise than so."—CARLYLE'S WORKS, Vol. VI., p. 214.

LONDON:

PRINTED FOR THE AUTHOR, AND TO BE HAD OF

J. DAVY AND SONS, 137, LONG ACRE.

1869.

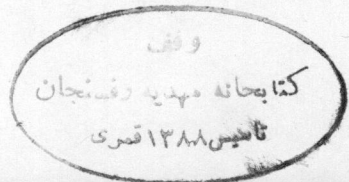

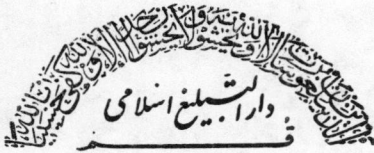

Exactly after a century !

The present book has been demanded by distinguished personalities, so we have been lucky to reproduce it in the present form, exactly after a complete century !

Although the present work has been considered the best essay about Islam, but as the author has not been a recognised muslim , there may be some defects in it, for which we are not responsible .

Moharam 1391
March 1971
Department of Publications
Darut—tablighe Islami . Ghum
IRAN

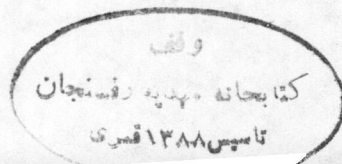

PREFACE.

———◆———

THE present work is an humble but earnest endea-
vour to free the history of Mohammed from false
accusations and illiberal imputations, and to vin-
dicate his just claim to be regarded as one of the
greatest benefactors of mankind.

The writers who, misguided by a blind zeal, have
thus assailed the fair fame of the Restorer of the
Worship of the UNITY, have not only shown themselves to be wholly uninfluenced by the spirit of that
charity so strongly and emphatically inculcated by the
Saviour himself, but have also erred in judgment, for
the least reflection would have convinced them that
it is not from a Christian and modern stand-point that
the Prophet and his doctrines ought to be examined
and criticised, but from an Eastern one; in other
words, Mohammed should be contemplated and judged
as a religious reformer and legislator living in Arabia
in the seventh century after Christ, and he must then,
most undoubtedly, be acknowledged as the very
greatest man whom Asia can claim as her son, if not,

one of the rarest and most transcendent geniuses the world itself ever produced.

If we consider what the Arabs were before Mohammed's appearance and what they became after it—if we reflect, moreover, upon the enthusiasm kindled and kept alive by his doctrine in the breasts of more than one hundred and sixty millions of the human race—we cannot but feel that to withhold our admiration from so extraordinary and so great a man would be the most flagrant injustice, and that to attribute his advent to mere blind chance would be to doubt the over-ruling power of Divine Providence.

In conclusion, the author would state that, in a few instances, when diffident of his own powers to do ample justice to so interesting and important a subject, he has availed himself of the ideas and language of other writers, an aid which he takes the present opportunity of candidly and gratefully acknowledging.

14, *Grove Terrace, St. John's Wood, London, N.W.*
August, 1869.

PART I.

LIFE OF MOHAMMED.

LIFE OF MOHAMMED.

————◆————

CHAPTER I.

It may be truly affirmed that of all known legislators and
conquerors, not one can be named, the history of whose
life has been written with greater authenticity and fuller
detail, than that of Mohammed. In fact, strip his biography
of the prodigies which Asiatic writers have ever affected,
and what remains may confidently defy incredulity itself.

At the period of Mohammed's birth a great part of
Arabia was under a foreign yoke; all the northern portion
of Arabia Petræa, as well as Syria, Palestine, and Egypt,
was under the sway of the Emperors of Constantinople.

B

The shores of the Persian Gulf, the countries watered by the Tigris and the Euphrates, and the southern provinces of the Peninsula, acknowledged the supremacy of the Chosroes of Persia. A portion of the coasts of the Red Sea to the south of Mecca was subject to the Christian kings of Abyssinia. Mecca and the all but inaccessible countries of the interior had preserved their independence. The political state of the country necessarily determined, to a great extent, the religious belief of the inhabitants. Thus, where the Greek and Abyssinian authority prevailed, there Christianity had the ascendancy ; the doctrines of the Magi and that of the Manicheans, both of which recognised two antagonistic principles, were predominant in the Persian provinces, while everywhere else idolatry held unbounded sway. In the first ages the Arabs had adored one supreme God (Allah Taala) creator of the heavens and the earth, but subsequently, had abandoned that worship and raised temples for the adoration of demons, sons of God, who, residing in the planets and fixed stars, governed the earth. These Gods were not universally adored throughout the country ; each tribe, each family had its particular divinities, its Lares, in fact, in honour of which even human victims were immolated. The Arabs believed neither in a future state nor in the creation of the world, but attributed the formation of the universe to nature, and its future destruction to time. Debauchery and robbery everywhere prevailed, and since death was regarded as the end, strictly so called, of existence, so was there neither recompense for virtue nor punishment for vice. A like moral and religious corruption was to be found among the Christians and the Jews who, for ages, had established themselves in the Arabian Peninsula, and had there formed very powerful parties. The Jews had come to seek in that land of liberty an asylum from the persecution of the Romans : the Christians had also fled thither in order to escape the massacres occasioned race, gave him on that account the name of Mohammed (*praised* or *most glorious*).*

The child was scarcely two years old when his father died, leaving him no other inheritance than two camels, a few sheep, and a female black slave named Barukut. His mother had hitherto suckled him, but cares and sorrows had dried up the fountains of her breast, and she therefore sought a nurse for him from among the Badwuna tribe. To succeed in this was, however, very difficult, for as these women always set a high price upon their services, they turned with contempt from this heir of poverty. At length, the wife of a Saadite shepherd, moved by compassion, took the helpless infant to her home in one of the villages near Mount Tayif, situated to the east of Mecca. He had not been long with these his foster-parents when their superstitious fears having been awakened by finding a mole between his shoulders, and which they attributed to the agency of the Djins or demons, they carried him back to his mother at Mecca.†

* Some Mohammedan writers assert that the performance of the rite of circumcision upon this infant was unnecessary, from his having been miraculously born without a foreskin. Goropius Becanus, in his 'Origines Antverpianæ,' relates the following curious circumstance respecting the foreskin of the Saviour. During the first crusade, Godefroi de Bouillon having heard that the women of Antwerp worshipped Priapus under the name of Ters, sent them the foreskin of Jesus Christ in the hope of its weaning them from so gross a superstition, but unfortunately without success.—The foreskins still extant of the Saviour are reckoned to be twelve in number: one was in the possession of the monks of Coulombs ; another at the Abbey of Charroux ; a third at Hildesheim, in Germany ; a fourth at Rome in the Church of St. Jean-de-Latran ; a fifth at Antwerp ; a sixth at Puyen Velay, in the church of Notre Dame, &c.

† Short as was the time he was with his foster-mother, Mohammed ever retained a grateful recollection of the kindness he had received from her. Halimà (that was the woman's name) visited him at Mecca, after his marriage with Khadijah. " It was," says tradition, " a year of drought, in which many cattle perished, and Mohammed spake unto Khadijah, and she gave to Halima a camel trained to carry a litter, and two score sheep, and she departed for her home with joyful heart." Upon another occasion, Mohammed spread his mantle for her to sit upon, in token of great regard, placing his hand upon her in a familiar and affectionate manner.

When Mohammed was six years old his mother died, on her return from a visit she and her son had paid to some relatives at Yathreb,* and was buried at Abwa, a village between Medina and Mecca. Nothing can give a better idea of the prophet's sensibility than the fact that her grave was a place of pious resort and tender recollections to her son to the latest hour of his existence. There is no doubt but that this early loss imparted to the youthful Mohammed somewhat of that pensive and meditative character which afterwards so distinguished him. In his seventh year he could appreciate the severity of his loss and feel the desolation of his orphan state, a subject to which he afterwards touchingly alludes in the Koran, when, reassuring his soul of the Divine favour and protection and recounting the mercies of the Almighty, he exclaims, " Did he not find thee an orphan and furnish thee with a refuge ? "†

At a subsequent period of his life, when on a pilgrimage from Medina to Hodaiba, he visited his mother's tomb, and some of his followers, who knew not that Amina lay buried there, seeing him weep sorely, inquired the cause : " This," replied he, " is my dear mother's grave ; the Lord hath permitted me to visit it ; I have sought permission to pray for her, but it has not been granted ; so, calling her to my remembrance, the tender recollection of her overcame me, and I wept."‡

After his mother's death, the care of the orphan devolved upon his paternal grandfather, Abd-el-Mutalleb, at that time high priest, and he also dying two years after, his son and

---

* This was the ancient name of Medina, which was chiefly inhabited by the tribes of the *Charegites* and the *Awsites*, and by two colonies of Jews of a sacerdotal race, and who by introducing among their Arab fellow citizens a taste for science and religion, had gained for that city the name of *the City of the Book*—that is, of the Prophet.

† Chapter xciii.

‡ This prohibition against praying for his mother's salvation forms a singular instance of the sternness and severity of the dogmas of Islam in respect of those who die in ignorance of the faith.

successor Abu Thaleb took the charge of the boy upon himself, treating him in every respect as one of his own children. It was now that Mohammed began to exhibit indications of an intelligent and inquiring mind. He loved to indulge in solitary meditation, so much so that when his playmates wished him to join in their amusements he replied, "Man is created for a nobler purpose than indulgence in frivolous pursuits." On Mohammed's attaining his thirteenth year, his uncle, who was a wealthy merchant, being on the eve of departing with the caravan for Syria, complied with his nephew's request to be allowed to accompany him, and the youth acquitted himself so well in this his first journey as to obtain no little credit. The next year he served in a military capacity, a circumstance which establishes the curious fact that the professions of the soldier and the trader, far from being considered by the Arabs as incompatible with each other, were frequently, among their most distinguished tribes, if not actually united, at least practised in rapid alternation. The active share taken by the youthful Mohammed in these expeditions developed in him both superior address and military talent, and the esteem and confidence procured him by these qualities were still more heightened by the sincerity of his words and actions, the regularity of his life, and the accuracy of his judgment. As he advanced in years, other merchants, gladly availing themselves of his great tact and ability, employed him as agent in their commercial transactions.

In one of the expeditions he made with his uncle, having arrived at a monastery in the Syrian desert, the superior of the establishment, fixing his scrutinizing gaze upon the face of the young traveller, took Abu Thaleb aside, saying, "Be very careful of thy nephew, and protect him from Jewish treachery, for truly he is born unto great things"—a prophetic warning, according to some writers, of the troubles and opposition which it was ordained the future prophet was to encounter from the descendants of Abraham.

It was while engaged in his commercial journeys that Mohammed frequented many of the various fairs held at different times in several parts of Arabia, and at which the popular traditions of the Arabs were recited, and the various religious faiths of the country expounded and enforced, and the experience he thus acquired upon these subjects convinced him more and more of the grossness and absurdity of the idolatry and degrading superstitions of his countrymen.

About this time the Kaaba, having been injured by fire, was undergoing repairs, in the course of which the sacred stone was to be replaced, and in order to avoid disputes, it was agreed that the honour of laying it, for the second time, should belong to him who first entered the sacred precincts; this was Mohammed, whom chance had conducted to the spot. He accordingly deposited the stone with all due ceremony, amid the acclamations of the bystanders, thus consecrating a temple devoted to the service of the very idols which it was afterwards the chief object of his mission to destroy; so that it was not merely a *stone* which he thus laid, but the foundation of a new religion of which he himself was to be the head and the pontiff.

Mohammed continued in his uncle's employment until his twenty-fifth year, when one of the leading men of the city, dying, and his widow, by name, Khadijah, requiring a factor to manage her business, he was recommended to her as a fit person for the purpose. Having accepted the terms she offered him, he traded for her during three years, at Damascus and other places, and upon returning to Mecca, proceeded to Khadijah's house that he might report to her in person the result of his commercial labours. The widow was highly satisfied with the balance-sheet; but there was a charm in the dark and pensive eye, in the noble features and graceful form of her assiduous agent, as he stood in a submissive attitude before her, which delighted her even more than did the increase of her wealth. The comely widow was at this time forty years of age, she had been twice married, and had borne two sons and a daughter, yet unable to resist the charm of so manly a person and the attractions of so sensible and enthusiastic a mind, it was not long ere she presented her hand to him in marriage.

At this time Mohammed was in the pride of manhood : his figure was commanding, his aspect majestic, his features regular and most expressive, his eyes black and piercing, his nose slightly aquiline, his mouth well formed and furnished with pearly teeth, while his cheeks were ruddy with robust health. Art had imparted to his naturally black flowing hair and beard a lighter chestnut hue. His captivating smile, his rich and sonorous voice, the graceful dignity of his gestures, the apparent frankness and heartiness of his manner, gained him the favourable attention of all whom he addressed. He possessed talents of a superior order—his perception was quick and active, his memory capacious and retentive, his imagination lively and daring, his judgment clear and perspicuous, his courage dauntless, and whatever may be the opinion of some as to the sincerity of his convictions, his tenacity of purpose in the pursuit of the great object of his life, and his patient endurance, cannot but extort the admiration of all. His natural eloquence was enhanced by the use of the purest dialect of Arabia, and adorned by the charm of a graceful elocution.

Not less favourable is the following description of Mohammed at a later period of his life, from the graphic pen of Gibbon :—" Mohammed was distinguished by the beauty of his person, an outward gift which is seldom despised, except by those to whom it has been refused. Before he spoke, the orator engaged on his side the affections whether of a public or a private audience. They applauded his commanding presence, his majestic aspect, his piercing eye, his gracious smile, his flowing beard, his countenance which painted every sensation of his soul, and the gestures that enforced each expression of the tongue. In the familiar offices of life, he scrupulously adhered to the grave and ceremonious politeness of his country; his respectful attention to the rich and powerful was dignified by his condescension and affability to the poorest citizen of Mecca; the frankness of his manner concealed the artifice of his views, and the habits of courtesy were imputed to personal friendship or universal benevolence; his memory was capacious and retentive, his wit easy and social, his imagination sublime, his judgment clear, rapid and decisive. He possessed the courage both of thought and action ;* and although his designs might gradually expand with success, the first idea which he entertained of his divine mission bears the stamp of an original and superior genius. The son of Abdallah was brought up in the bosom of the noblest race, in the use of the purest dialect of Arabia, and the fluency of his speech was corrected and enhanced by the practice of discreet and seasonable silence."

As to acquired learning, in the common acceptation of the word, it is confessed that Mohammed had none at all,* having had no other education than what was customary in his tribe, who neglected and, perhaps, despised what we call literature, esteeming no language in comparison with their own, their skill in which they gained by use and not by books, contenting themselves, moreover, with improving their private experience by committing to memory such passages of their poets as they judged might be of use to them in active life. The Arab, therefore, who never had a

---

* Moses and Mohammed were not men of speculation ; they were men of action. It was in proposing action to their fellow countrymen and to their contemporaries, that they governed humanity." (Renan, 'Life of Jesus,' chap. iv.)

† See Suras, chapters vii., xxix., xcvi.

teacher was often, nevertheless, a very superior man, for the tent is a kind of school always open, where, from the contact with men of experience and ability, there is produced a great intellectual and even literary movement. What we call education has nothing in common with the refinement of manners and the acuteness of intellect of the Orientals.

The story of Mohammed's marriage as told by Arab writers is, in the highest degree, graceful and interesting, the nuptials being celebrated with extraordinary magnificence; two camels were slain for the entertainment, and Khadijah's slaves danced to the sound of timbrels to amuse the guests.

At the time of his marriage, Mohammed was twenty-eight years of age, and his wife forty, though still beautiful, but, notwithstanding this great disparity of years, he seems to have lived in the most affectionate manner with his benefactress, never having availed himself of his country's law, which allowed him to have other wives, at discretion.

A period of fifteen years now occurs, during which the Prophet's history remains obscure and impenetrable. Such was the interval during which Jesus worked in the shop of Joseph the carpenter;* a sacred interval in which the man may be said to have assisted at the birth of his own genius, preparing in silence and maturing by meditation, the mission entrusted to him by the Almighty. To purify his life and render it unassailable by censure or malice, was now Mohammed's constant and anxious solicitude and occupation. Every year he is said to have passed one month in a grotto of Mount Hara, about three leagues to the west of Mecca; and here it was that he studied the Bible and the Gospels, indulged his contemplative disposition, and enjoyed the luxury of meditation. Such intense occupation of the

---

* " He (Jesus) followed the trade of his father, which was that of a carpenter. This was not, in any degree, humiliating or grievous. The Jewish custom required that a man devoted to intellectual work should learn a trade." (Renan, 'Life of Jesus,' chap. v.)

mind on one subject, accompanied by fervent enthusiasm of spirit, could not but have a powerful effect upon his frame. He became subject to dreams, ecstasies and trances.* For six months successively, according to one of his biographers, he had constant dreams bearing upon the subject of his waking thoughts.

What was the real character of Mohammed's ecstatic periods; whether they were simply reveries of profound meditation, or swoons connected with a morbid excitability of the mental or physical constitution, it would be difficult to determine; but certain it is that at the moment of inspiration, anxiety pressed upon him and his countenance was troubled. He would fall to the ground like one intoxicated or overcome with sleep, and, on the coldest day, his forehead would be bedewed with big drops of perspiration. Nay, it is even asserted that if he happened to be astride his camel when so excited, the animal would itself become affected by a wild restlessness—now falling upon her haunches, then starting up again; at one time fixing her feet rigidly in the ground, and anon throwing her legs about as if wishing to rid herself of them.

The assertion, so often repeated, that Mohammed was subject to epileptic fits, is a base invention of the Greeks, who would seem to *impute* that morbid affection to the apostle of a novel creed as a stain upon his moral character deserving the reprobation and abhorrence of the Christian world. Surely, those malignant bigots might have reflected that if Mohammed had really been afflicted with that dreadful malady Christian charity ought to have commanded them to pity his misfortune rather than rejoice over it, or affect to regard it in the light of a sign of Divine wrath.

---

* " Mohammed was sorrowful in temperament; continually meditating : he had no rest; he never spoke except from necessity; he used to be long silent; he opened and ended his speech from the corners of his mouth; he expressed himself in pregnant sentences, using neither too few, nor too many words." (From the ' Kâtib al Wâckidi,' p. 81½.)

It was in the fortieth year of his life, that while passing, as above described, the month of Ramadhan,* he lay wrapped in his mantle during the silent watches of the night, that he heard a voice calling him by name. Uncovering his head, there suddenly broke in upon him a flood of light of such intolerable splendour and intensity that he swooned away. On recovering his senses, an angel, in human form, approaching him, displayed to his view a silken cloth covered with writing :—

"Read!" said the angel.

"I know not how to read."†

"Read, in the name of Allah, the Creator of all things, who made man from a clot of blood! Read, in the name of the Most High, who taught man the use of the *kullam* (pen), and who can dart into his soul the beams of knowledge."

Mohammed's mind was instantaneously illumined, and he read, with ease, the writing on the silken cloth; then, under the influence of an irresistible excitement, he rushed forth and plunged into the innermost recesses of the forest, from all sides whereof he heard a voice crying aloud,— "Mohammed! thou art the Apostle of God the Most High, and I, I am the angel Gabriel."

If it be considered that it is by no means uncommon for the mind when in solitude, to embody, as it were, the phantoms of the imagination, and to mistake its own creations for absolute existences, and, moreover, that men, and sometimes women, even of the strongest intellect, are particularly liable to such impressions, as in the case of the ghost of Cæsar in the tent of Brutus,‡ the gigantic figure which fore-

---

* The word *Ramadhan* comes from *ramad* (burning), the month being so called because, in the solar year of the ancient Arabs, it occurred at the time of the greatest heats.

† See page 12, note †.

‡ "Thus, a little before he (Brutus) left Asia, he was sitting alone in his tent, by a dim light, and at a late hour, the whole army lay in sleep and silence, while the general, wrapt in meditation, thought he perceived something enter his tent; turning towards the door, he saw a horrible and monstrous spectre standing silently by his side." (Langhorne's 'Plutarch').

told Cromwell's greatness; * and in later times, Molinos,†
Madame de Guyon,‡ Swedenborg,§ and Madame Krudner,∥
it becomes more than probable that so far from Mohammed
having been guilty of a falsehood in afterwards announcing
that the angel Gabriel commanded him to undertake the
prophetic mission, he really and conscientiously believed
himself to be the divinely inspired Apostle of God.

On the morning of the 24th Ramadan, Mohammed ap-

* Many stories are told of Cromwell's enthusiasm in this, the early part
of his life, one of which we shall mention. Lying melancholy upon his
bed, in the daytime, he fancied he saw a spectre, which told him he
should be the greatest man in the kingdom." (Chalmers's 'Biographical
Dictionary').

† Molinos, a Spaniard, was born at Saragossa, and was the author of that
species of mysticism called *Quietism*, a system afterwards espoused in
France by Madame Guyon and the virtuous Fénelon, Archbishop of Cambray.
He taught, in his ' Spiritual Guide,' that the pious mind must possess
quietude in order to secure its spiritual progress ; that for this purpose it
must be abstracted from visible objects ; that being thus drawn within
itself, it becomes susceptible of heavenly influence ; and that the special
functions of the intellect and of the will are merged wholly in God. Molinos
was thrown into prison in 1685 on account of these doctrines, and notwithstanding his recantation of them, he was in 1687 condemned to perpetual
imprisonment, and died, unreleased, in 1697.

‡ Madame de Guyon was born at Montargis in 1648. The amiable
Fénelon and Madame de Maintenon were converts to her doctrines, which
reduced all religion to a pure love of God. After six years' imprisonment
at the instigation of Bossuet, she was banished to Diziers, near Blois, and
died there in 1717.

§ Swedenborg was born at Stockholm in 1688. His vast acquirements in
general literature and natural philosophy procured him a European reputation, and he became a member of several learned societies. Suddenly seized
in 1745 with the conviction that he was destined to regenerate Christianity,
he declared that, warned by a divine appearance, he would abandon his
uncompleted studies, and devote himself to the new office to which he was
called. He imagined that he not only saw and discoursed with spirits, but
that he actually lived with them as a spirit, seeing all things in the spirit
world, as one of themselves. He died in 1772.

∥ A celebrated mystic, born in 1784, and who, after living a very dissi-
pated life, gave herself up to an extravagant devotion, imagining that she
had a mission from heaven to regenerate Christianism. In 1815 she
obtained so great an influence over the Emperor of Russia, Alexander I., as
to have had a great share in the formation of the " Holy Alliance." She
died in the Crimea in 1824.

peared before his wife, apparently, greatly disturbed in mind. He called out to her to "wrap him up, to affuse him with cold water, as his soul was greatly troubled!" and having recovered himself, proceeded to break to his amazed spouse the secret of his divine mission. Nor did she hesitate one moment to believe it implicitly; and no wonder, for Mohammed, to his honour be it written, had proved a most kind and attentive husband to her whose affection had raised him above the pressure of want. He had abstained, and, till her death, continued to abstain from availing himself of the right of polygamy. He had proved his *truth* to her by unvarying affection: how, then, could she possibly have doubted his word? She therefore regarded and believed the vision to be a real manifestation of God's will.* The next converts were Zeid, his Arab slave, to whom he granted his freedom, and his own cousin, Ali, the son of Abu-Thaleb. He then addressed himself, and with complete success, to Abu-Bekr,† a man of wealth and influence among the Koreish, and by his example and exhortations other principal inhabitants of Mecca became converted to the new faith.

It is strongly corroborative of Mohammed's sincerity that the earliest converts to Islam were his bosom friends and the people of his household, who, all intimately acquainted with his private life, could not fail otherwise to have detected those discrepancies which more or less invariably exist between the pretentions of the hypocritical deceiver and his actions at home.

But a check soon followed this first success, for having convened a meeting of the chief members of his tribe,

---

* "I do not remember to have read," says Sale ('Prel. Disc.,' p. 58, note 3), "in any Eastern writer that Khadijah ever rejected her husband's pretences as delusions, or suspected him of imposture."

† Abu-Bekr's original name was *Abdel-Kaaba* (servant of the Kaaba); this he afterwards changed for that of Abdallah, but after giving his daughter Ayesha to the Prophet, in marriage, he assumed, as an honourable distinction, the name of *Abu-Bekr* (father of the Virgin).

Mohammed no sooner declared to them his mission than the announcement was received with coldness and incredulity, but when, not content with insisting upon the unity of the Godhead and his own Apostleship, he informed his auditors that it was his intention to overthrow idolatry and bring his countrymen back to the religion of Abraham, their indignation burst forth from all sides, and it was proposed to silence him at once ; nor were any more violent in this their opposition than the other families of his own tribe. Abu-Thaleb, however, though he did not become a convert, still continued his protection to his nephew.

For the next few years Mohammed's life was passed in a state of persecution and insult, which extended itself to his few disciples. Once, indeed, his adversaries made offers of wealth or of leadership if he would abandon his purpose ; but he replied by reciting that portion of the Koran known as the 41st Chapter, and from which the following are a few extracts :—

" A revelation from the Compassionate, the Merciful ! I am but a man like unto you. It is revealed unto me that your God is *one* God ; go straight then unto Him and implore His pardon. And woe to such as join Gods with Gods :

" Who pay not the alms of obligation, and in the life to come, believe not :

" But they who believe and do the things that are right, shall, assuredly, receive a perfect never failing recompence.

" Do ye, indeed, disbelieve in Him who, in two days, created the earth ? and do ye assign unto Him, peers ? The Lord of the Worlds is He !

" He hath placed on the earth the firm mountains which above it tower ; and He hath blessed it, and in four days distributed food throughout it, for the cravings of all.

" Next did He apply Himself unto the Heavens which then were but smoke ; and to them and the earth did he say:

' Come ye, whether in accordance with or against your will,' and they both replied : ' We come, obedient.'

" If a lure from Satan entice thee, then take thou refuge in God, for He is the Hearing, the Knowing.

" Falsehood, from whatsoever side it cometh, shall not approach. It (the Koran) is a missive sent down from the Wise, the Praise-worthy.

" Nothing hath been said to thee (Mohammed) which hath not been said o old to apostles before thee. Verily, with thy Lord is forgiveness and with Him is terrible retribution."

Mohammed's opponents answered this by requiring him to work a miracle in proof of his Divine mission : but he refused, saying that he was sent to preach truth, not to work miracles; appealing, at the same time, to the Koran, he challenged his adversaries to produce any work that could rival it in beauty and sublimity.*

No proof, indeed, has ever been adduced that Mohammed at any time descended to any artifices or pseudo-miracles to enforce his doctrines or establish his apostolic claims. He appears on the contrary to have relied entirely upon reason and eloquence, and to have been supported by religious enthusiasm in this earlier stage of his career. Religious enthusiasm was, in fact, Mohammed's ruling passion; it appeared in his every action, and displayed itself in every stage of his existence.

It is singular that although Mohammed so expressly disclaimed all miraculous powers, yet every kind of miracles has been fathered upon him, and that the true history and the true teaching of the prophet should have been as much

---

* " And if ye be in doubt as to that which We (God) have sent down unto our servant (Mohammed), then produce a chapter like unto it " (chap. ii). Mohammed considered the unprecedented union of the Arabs, under him, as testifying the truth of his mission, for he says in chapter viii., " If thou (Mohammed) hadst expended whatever riches are on the earth, thou could'st not have united their hearts, but God united them, for He is mighty and wise."

disfigured by fable and comments, as the history and teaching of any Christian saint. In fact, the notices in the Koran are almost as unlike the legendary history of Mohammed as the narrative of the Gospels differs from the fanciful ideas of Buonaventura.*

Gibbon has favoured us with the following account of one of these attributed marvels :—

"The Christians, rashly enough, have ascribed to Mohammed a tame pigeon that seemed to descend from Heaven and whisper in his ear. As this pretended miracle was brought forward by Grotius (*De veritate religionis Christianæ*), his Arab translator, the learned Pococke, inquired of him the names of his authors, and Grotius was obliged to confess that it was unknown to the Mohammedans themselves. Lest, however, it should provoke their indignation and ridicule, the *pious lie* was suppressed in the Arabic version, but still maintains a conspicuous place in the numerous editions of the Latin text.†

Seeing that Mohammed's enemies still remained most inveterate against him, Abu-Thaleb earnestly dissuaded his nephew from pursuing his purpose any further, but his reply was, "Though the Koreishites should arm against me, the sun and the moon (alluding to the divinities which they ignorantly worshipped), the one on my right hand and the other on my left, I would not be shaken from my resolution."

Nothing daunted, therefore, by opposition, he again assembled a few guests, chiefly belonging to his own tribe, placed before them, it is said, a lamb and a bowl of milk, and, after the frugal meal, rose up, declared his sacred character, offered the treasures of time and of eternity to whomsoever should become his disciples, and concluded an

---

* A celebrated doctor of the Catholic Church, born in 1221. He became general of the Franciscan order. His works, remarkable for their mysticism, procured him the appellation of the *Seraphic* Doctor.

† Gibbon, ' Decline and Fall,' vol. v. p. 511 (note). Bohn's edition.

address remarkable for its native eloquence, by the demand, " Who among you will aid me to bear this burden ?   Who will be my lieutenant and vizier, as Aaron was to Moses ?"

The assembly remained mute with astonishment, not one venturing to accept the proffered perilous office, until the young and impetuous Ali, Mohammed's cousin, started up, exclaiming, " O prophet ! I will ; though I am, indeed, the youngest of these present, the most rheumy of them as to eyes, the biggest of them as to belly, and the slenderest of them as to legs.   I, O prophet ! will be thy Vizier over them !"

On which, throwing his arms around the generous youth, and pressing him to his bosom, Mohammed exclaimed, " Behold, my brother, my Vizier !"*

Having thus made a commencement, Mohammed began to preach publicly in Mecca, daily adding to the number of his disciples, his favourite places for preaching being the hills of Safa and Kubeis, in the neighbourhood of the above city ; but he still made occasional visits to Mount Hara, returning thence with fresh suras or chapters for the book subsequently known as the Koran.

It was about this time that he acquired a new and important convert in the person of Omar, one of the most uncompromising but most generous of his enemies.   Omar had been already highly displeased with his sister, Ameina, for having embraced the new faith, so that finding her one day reading the Koran aloud, he struck her violently, dashing, at the same time, the book on the ground.   The maiden, calm and collected, picked up the volume, but still persisted in refusing to give it to her brother, who, now still more exasperated, snatched it from her, but his eye glancing involuntarily over some of its lines, he was

* Some writers render Ali's words thus :—" I will beat out the teeth, pull out the eyes, rip up the bellies, and break the legs of all who oppose thee ;" a mistake which originated in the mis-translation of the original by Gagnier in his ' Life of Abu-el-Teda.'

seized with wonder, and conviction succeeding to admiration, he became a Mussulman on the spot. He then immediately ran, armed as he was, to the castle of Safa, the asylum of Mohammed, who, upon seeing him approach, exclaimed, "Whence comest thou, O Omar! Wilt thou remain here until crushed beneath the vaulted roof that will fall upon thee?" "I come," replied Omar, "a true believer in the true God, and in thee, his chosen apostle!"

The Koreish, finding that Mohammed still zealously persisted in the promulgation of his doctrines, tried what they could do by violence, treating his followers so cruelly that it was not safe for them to continue at Mecca, whereupon Mohammed gave permission to such as had not friends to protect them to seek for refuge elsewhere, which they did, and found it in Abyssinia. This first *hegira,* or, more properly, *hedjira* (flight) took place in the fifth year of Mohammed's mission. The number of the refugees amounted successively to eighty men and women and a few children. The fugitives were kindly received by the Nejashee, or king of the country, who refused to deliver them up to the parties sent by the Koreish to demand their extradition, becoming himself, as Arabian writers assert, a convert to Islam.

CHAPTER II.

IN the second year of his mission, Mohammed's party
growing powerful and formidable at Mecca, the city passed
a decree forbidding any more citizens to become his followers. This, however, did not much affect him while his
uncle Abu-Thaleb lived to protect him, but he dying two
years after, Mohammed's position became very critical, inasmuch as the property and influence of that relative passed
into the hands of his (Mohammed's) enemies, who, being
now more powerful than ever, were the more inveterate
against him, insulting him upon every occasion, even while
he was at prayers, throwing all sorts of filth upon his food,
and harassing him with every other kind of contumely. To
add to these misfortunes, Thaleb had only been dead a few
days when the prophet's faithful wife Khadijah expired in

his arms. The death of this his beloved partner was indeed a heart-rending calamity for him. For twenty years she had been his counsellor and supporter, and now his soul and his hearth had become desolate. Notwithstanding that at so advanced an age she must have lost every youthful charm, yet Mohammed had remained faithful to her to the last, and refrained, as already said, from taking other wives.

Khadijah was buried in the cemetery at Mecca, situated to the north-west of the city; and we learn from Burckhardt, the celebrated traveller, that her tomb is still remaining and is regularly visited by pilgrims, especially on Friday mornings, but that it presents no object of curiosity except the tombstone, which has a fine inscription in Cufic characters, containing a passage from the chapter of the Koran entitled Souret-ul-Kursy.

Mohammed's gratitude to her memory survived her to his latest hour. The tenderness of this his recollection of her having aroused the reproachful and insolent jealousy of Ayesha, the most youthful and blooming of the wives who had replaced her—"Was she not old, and has not Heaven given thee a fairer and a better?" "No, before God!" cried Mohammed, in a burst of generous emotion, "there never was a better or a kinder helpmate: she believed in me when I was despised and mocked of men; she comforted and relieved me when I was poor, despised and persecuted by the world."

The persecution to which Mohammed was now subjected, wholly unprotected as he was, from such even of the Koreish who were his near relations, or who had at one time been his friends, compelled him to seek a place of refuge; so that, followed by his faithful Zeid, he fled to the small town of Tayif, about sixty miles to the east of Mecca, and where resided another uncle of his, by name, Abbas. Upon arriving there he immediately addressed himself to three principal men of the place, explaining his mission and inviting them to merit the honour of supporting the new faith and assisting him in propagating it, but he failed in producing conviction; they cast in his teeth the common objections of his own people, and advised him to seek protection elsewhere. He, however, remained there for one month, and was treated with some little respect by the better disposed and more considerate of the people, but at length the slaves and the lower classes rose against him, pelted him with stones, and chased him for two or three miles across the sandy plain as far as the foot of the hills that surround the city. There, weary and exhausted, he took refuge in one of the numerous orchards and rested himself for some time under a vine; after which he resumed his journey to Mecca, and having arrived in its vicinity, despatched a message to Mota' ab Ebn Adi, a man of much influence, and who was favourably disposed to him, entreating that he would secure a safe entrance for him into the city. His request was granted. Mota' ab assembled his sons and retainers, ordering them to take their stand, armed, by the Kaaba. Upon which Mohammed and Zeid entered Mecca, his protector forbidding that any ill treatment or violence should be offered them; and the prophet, then advancing, kissed the sacred stone and returned to his house, escorted by Mota' ab and his party.

About two months after the death of Khadijah, Mohammed married Sawda, a widow, and nearly at the same time Ayesha, the young and beautiful daughter of his bosom friend Abu-Bekr, the principal object of this last union being to cement still more strongly their mutual attachment.

Mohammed is said to have taken after the death of Khadijah, at different periods, eleven or twelve wives, out of fifteen or thirteen who had been betrothed to him, and he is constantly upbraided on this account by the controversial writers who adduce this circumstance as a demonstrative proof of his sensuality. But over and above the consideration that polygamy, though it is forbidden by European law, was in Mohammed's time generally practised in Arabia and other parts of the East, and was far from being counted an immorality, it should be recollected that he lived from the age of five-and-twenty to that of fifty years satisfied with one wife; that until she died at the age of sixty-three he took no other, and that she left him without male issue; and it may then be asked, is it likely that a very sensual man, of a country where polygamy was a common practice, should be contented for five-and-twenty years with one wife, she being fifteen years older than himself; and is it not far more probable that Mohammed took the many wives he did during the last thirteen years of his life chiefly from a desire of having male issue?

The sacred month in which the caravans of pilgrims came to Mecca was a season of universal peace; while it lasted the fiercest animosities were suspended, and crowds came fearlessly from every quarter to celebrate the annual jubilee in the national temple. Mohammed eagerly seized so favourable an opportunity for preaching to the assembled multitudes, and gained several proselytes, inhabitants of Yahtreb, and who on their return home spoke in high commendation of the new religion, zealously exhorting their friends and fellow-citizens to embrace the same, and their success was the greater from the fact of the new religion being unpopular at Mecca, for commercial jealousy had excited a spirit of rivalry between the two cities.

In the twelfth year of his mission Mohammed related the history of his night journey (*maraj*) to Jerusalem, and thence to heaven, on the creature called El Barak, and under the guidance of the angel Gabriel, and respecting which the Koran contains some obscure intimation in Chapter xvii.*

---

* The passage is as follows : " Praise be to Him who carried his servant by night from the Sacred Temple to the farther Temple, the environs of

The account, as given by the prophet, was, that one night as he was asleep by the side of his wife Ayesha, he heard a knocking at his door, upon which, having arisen, he found there the angel Gabriel, and standing close to him Al Barak, a mysterious animal, with a human face, the ears of an elephant, the neck of a camel, the body of a horse, the tail of a mule, and the hoofs of a bullock; in colour he was as white as milk; and his swiftness equalled that of lightning itself. The angel, now expanding his seventh pair of wings, took flight, and the prophet, mounted upon Al Barak, followed him. Arrived at Jerusalem, Mohammed met there Abraham, Moses and Jesus Christ, whom he saluted, calling them brothers, and uniting with them in prayer. After this, leaving Jerusalem with Gabriel, Mohammed found a ladder of light ready fixed for them, and which they immediately ascended, having first fastened El Barak to an iron ring rivetted in the solid rock, that he might await their return. Having reached the celestial abodes, Gabriel introduced his companion successively, as Virgil did Dante,* into the different heavens, seven in number, and on his entering the first one, Mohammed saw a multitude of angels of all manner of shapes—some in that of a *man*, others in that of *birds*, and others in that of *beasts* of every description; and among the birds he saw a cock of enormous size and with plumage as white as snow; all the angels having come from the earth to intercede with God for all the living creatures dwelling thereon. At length the travellers penetrated to where the sacred Lotus tree stands, marking the

which we have blessed, that we might show him some of our signs. Verily, he it is that heareth and seeth." A fuller narrative of this night-journey will be found in Taylor's ' History of Mohammedanism,' Appendix ii. p. 334.

* " Ond' io per lo tuo me' penso e discerno
  Che tu mi segni, ed io sarò tua guida.
  'Dell' Inferno,' canto primo, l. 112 & 113.
  (I for thy profit pondering now devise,
  Will lead thee hence, and be to thee a guide.)

limit to the garden of delights ; the fruits of this tree being
so enormously large that one only would suffice to feed for
an immense length of time, all created beings.　Here they
met with a barrier hitherto impassable to any mortal, and
which separates the heavens from the Almighty's throne.
At the Lotus tree a new angelic guide was awaiting them,
by whom Mohammed was led over infinite tracts of space
and through myriads of celestial intelligencies incessantly
employed in singing the praises of God.　At length he
entered the beatific presence, and was permitted to approach within two bows' length of the throne of the Most
High, on which he beheld, graven in characters of flaming
fire, the formula he afterwards adopted as the symbol
of his faith—" There is no God but God, and Mohammed is
his Apostle."　The words spoken by the Almighty to His
servant could not be revealed ; all we are told is, that God
ordered that Mussulmans should pray fifty times a day, but
that the prophet, by the advice of Moses, begged that the
number might be reduced to five, a request which was
granted.

Rejoining Gabriel, both of them set forth on their return
to Mecca.　At Jerusalem the prophet remounted Barak,
and was by that animal brought safe home again.　So
brief a portion of mundane time having, according to some
commentators, been consumed in this so marvellous a journey, that a pitcher full of water, accidentally overturned by
Mohammed when rising from his bed to join Gabriel, had
not reached the floor on his return ; so that he actually
replaced it ere a single drop had been spilled.

This narrative of the "night journey" is one in which
tradition revels with congenial ecstasy.　The rein has
been given loose to a pious imagination.　Both the journey and the ascent to Heaven are decked out in the most
extravagant colouring of romance, and in all the gorgeous
drapery that fancy could conceive.

There was much dispute among Mohammed's followers upon the subject of the "night-journey;" some asserted that it was nothing but a vision or dream,* others† that the prophet was conveyed bodily to Jerusalem, and that the spirit only ascended thence to Heaven; and others, that he performed both the night-journey to Jerusalem and the ascension to Heaven, in his body. This last opinion was the most prevalent, and it seems that Mohammed did not deny its correctness.‡ In the same year in which the maraj or night-journey is said to have occurred, and which is called by Mohammedans the *accepted year*, twelve men of Yahtreb came to Mecca and took an oath of fidelity to the prophet at Akaba, a hill to the north of that city. This oath was called the *Women's oath*, not that any women were present at the time, but because it was the same oath that was afterwards exacted of the women : viz., that they should not steal nor commit fornication, nor kill their children (as the pagan Arabs did whenever they apprehended that they should not be able to maintain them), nor forge calumnies, and that they should obey the Prophet in all things reasonable.

Whilst Mohammed's nocturnal journey was the subject of warm discussion at Mecca, Yahtreb resounded with his praises, and crowds repaired to him; from among whom he retained awhile twelve for the purpose of instructing them in the new faith, after which they were sent back to

* Ayesha declared that it must have been a dream, Mohammed having been in bed with her throughout the night on which the journey was said to have been performed.

† The Sonnites, and among them the pious Al Jannabi, declare, in an article of faith, that to deny the nocturnal journey of the Prophet is to disbelieve the Koran.

‡ The ridicule and sarcasm in which many Christian writers have indulged on the subject of this narrative, are, to say the least, injudicious, as being equally applicable to the visions of Jacob. (Genesis, chap. xvii. 11 and 12 ; Ezekiel, chap. i. 4 to 29 inclusive ; chap. iv. 12 to 15 inclusive ; Daniel, chap. vii. *passim ;* Acts of the Apostles, chap. ix. 3, 6, 9 ; Revelations, *passim.*)

the above city as his twelve apostles, there to propagate Islamism. In this they laboured so successfully as in a short time to draw over to the new faith the greater part of the inhabitants; a circumstance of which Mohammed was no sooner informed than he resolved to repair thither immediately, the more so as Abu Sophian, the Prophet's inveterate and implacable foe, had succeeded Abu-Thaleb as Governor of Mecca; and as it had, moreover, been determined by the Koreish to employ assassins with the view of ridding themselves of an enemy whose popularity and influence were daily increasing.

The secret of this conspiracy being betrayed to Mohammed, he and his friend Abu-Bekr escaped in the silence and darkness of the night, Ali being directed to lie down in his place and cover himself with the Prophet's well-known green mantle. After surrounding the house, the assassins then forcibly entered it, but finding, instead of their purposed victim, the youthful Ali, calmly and resignedly awaiting the death intended for his chief, so much devotedness excited the pity even of those men of blood, and Ali was left unharmed.

In the meantime, Mohammed and his friend had taken refuge in one of the caves of Mount Thor, at a short distance from Mecca, and here they remained three days, Abu-Bekr's son and daughter bringing them intelligence and supplies of food. While thus lying concealed, Abu-Bekr, seeing the Prophet in such great peril, became very dejected, and said, " How can we escape, for we are but two?" "Not so," replied Mohammed, "for there is yet a third, God himself, and He will protect us." The assassins, still continuing the pursuit, arrived before the cavern, but seeing at its entrance a pigeon's nest crossed by a spider's web (both miraculously placed there), they concluded the cave to be empty and renewed their search in a different direction. On this Mohammed and his companion left the cave, and, taking a by-road, arrived safely at Yahtreb, whither Ali followed them three days afterwards. This second flight or emigration (*hegira*) took place on the 16th of July, A.D. 622, thirteen years after Mohammed had announced his mission, and during the reign of Khosrou Paranis in Persia,* the Prophet being at the time fifty-three years old. Mohammed was enthusiastically welcomed at Yahtreb, the citizens, in honour of him, changing this ancient name of their city to that of *Medenat-el Nabi* (the city of the prophet).

At Medina he assumed the sacerdotal and regal office and there, leaning against a palm-tree, or in a rough, unadorned pulpit, he inveighed against the idolatry of his nation, breathing into his hearers such a spirit of zeal, enthusiasm and devotedness that, both in the camp and without the walls of the city, the ambassadors from Mecca were compelled to confess that he was treated with greater respect, and commanded more implicit obedience than even the Chosroes of Persia or the Cæsars of Constantinople.

Hitherto the new religion had been exclusively doctrinal, but it now became necessary to place it upon a firm and unalterable basis, to devise forms of worship, and institute practical observances, and accordingly, Mohammed appointed the daily prayers, the hour at which they were to be recited, and the point of the heavens toward which the faithful were to turn in their worship.† At this time also

---

* This flight, or emigration, was not, as we have seen, the first, but it was the most famous. The Hegira was first appointed by Omar, the third Caliph or Emperor of the Saracens, and dates, as is said in the text, from the 16th of July, 622. Indeed, the day that Mohammed left Mecca was on the first of the preceding Rabia, and he came to Medina on the 12th of the same month, that is on the 12th of our September; but the Hegira begins two months before, from the 1st of Moharram; for that being the first month of the Arabian year, Omar would make no alteration as to that, but anticipated the computation 59 days, that he might commence his era from the beginning of that year in which the flight of Mohammed happened, and from which it took its name.

† Among the Eastern nations, this point is called the *Kebla*. Among the

the first mosque was built, a structure of the simplest and most unpretending character; Mohammed worked at it with his own hands. Now, likewise, was introduced the custom of summoning the faithful to prayers by *muezin* (criers), who, ascending one of the minarets cried aloud with stentorian voice, " God is great; there is no God but one, and Mohammed is his prophet. Come to prayers ! God is great, and the only one !"* Mohammed may now be regarded as uniting in his own person the offices of monarch, general, judge, and priest; his Divine inspiration was generally acknowledged, nor ever was there devotedness equal to that received by him from his followers ; so great, indeed, was the reverence paid him, that whatever had touched his person was deemed sacred. But, although possessed of more than imperial power, nothing could exceed the prophet's simple style of living; thus, we are told by Ayesha, that he swept out his own chamber, lit his own fire, and mended his own clothes ; that his food consisted of dates and barley bread, with milk and honey, which were supplied to him by the charity of the faithful.†

But while thus engaged in spiritual matters, the prophet's attention was not the less directed to secular ones. Having received intelligence that a rich caravan of a thousand camels, and under the command of Abu Sophian, was coming from Syria, and for whose protection the Meccans had sent an escort of 950 chosen men, Mohammed resolved to attack it, although he could muster only 313 soldiers, sixty camels, and two horses. He took post near the well of Bedr, on

Jews it was towards the temple of Jerusalem ; the Mohammedans towards the Kaába of Mecca ; the Sabians towards the meridian ; and the Magians towards the *rising* sun.

* Mohammed instituted this custom, as he considered that of summoning believers to prayer by means of the sound of drums and trumpets, or by that of the ringing of bells, as among the Christians, unsuitable to the solemnity of the occasion.

† " God," says Al Bokhari, " offered him the treasures of the earth, but he would not accept them."

the Mecca road, not far from the Red Sea, and had scarcely drawn up his troops in order of battle when the advanced column of the Meccans appeared over the rising sands in front, but their greatly superior numbers were concealed by the fall of the ground behind. Mohammed was perfectly alive to his critical situation, and well knowing, as he did, that the very fate of Islam hung upon the issue, he lifted up his hands to Heaven, and poured forth these earnest prayers : —"O Lord, I beseech thee, forget not thy promise both of aid and of victory ! O Lord, should this little band be discomfited, idolatry will prevail, and the pure and true worship of Thee cease throughout the earth !" And now began the deadly contest, in the midst of which the prophet, with fire-flashing eyes and loud voice, declared the gates of paradise open to all who should die in the sacred cause of God. "The angels," shouted he, "are on our side. I see them advancing towards us ! Hark ! I hear the angel Gabriel calling his charger Hissoum ! it is the sword of God which smiteth !" Then, stooping down and taking up a handful of sand, he cast it towards the Meccans, exclaiming, "Let their faces be confounded !" The enthusiastic fury of the Moslems proved irresistible, and Mohammed returned victorious to Medina, where the immense spoil he had taken was equally divided among his faithful followers. The battle of Bedr is frequently mentioned in the Koran, and it is to the prestige it gave Mohammed that he was largely indebted for his subsequent success.

The next year, A.D. 624, the fierce resentment of Abu Sophian and of the Koreish brought into the field, against Mohammed, a body of 3000 men headed by Abu Sophian, who advanced to within six miles of Medina, where he encountered the Prophet at the head of 950 followers on Mount Ahed.* The Koreish advanced in the form of a crescent,

---

* *Ahed* signifies *one* ; this name being given to the mountain on account of its standing isolated in the plain.

the right wing of the cavalry being led by Kaled, the fiercest and most redoubtable of the Arab warriors. Mohammed had made his dispositions with considerable skill; his troops were successfnl at first and broke the enemy's centre; but their eagerness for spoil threw their ranks into disorder, and Kaled immediately attacked them in the flank and rear. Mohammed was wounded in the face with a javelin, and two of his teeth were shattered by a stone. Kaled exclaimed with a loud voice that the lying prophet was slain, upon which, without stopping to ascertain the truth, the followers of Islam fled panic-stricken, while a few of the most devoted adherents of the prophet gathered round him and conveyed him to a place of safety. In order to reward the heroism displayed by his cousin Ali in this fierce and disastrous engagement, Mohammed gave him, in marriage, his beloved daughter Fatima, a maiden of such rare beauty and virtue that the Arabs included her in the number of the four holy women—Pharaoh's wife, the Virgin Mary, Khadijah and herself.

The year after this marriage, Mohammed instituted the feast of Ramadan.* † About this time several Arab tribes pretending to have been converted to Islam, desired Mohammed to send them two of his disciples for the purpose of instructing them in the doctrines of his religion, but the missionaries had no sooner arrived than they were treacherously and cruelly murdered. The Jews, likewise,

---

* See page 15, note *.

† The punishment assigned by Mohammed for the violation of this fast is particularly lenient and reasonable : " And those who can keep it (the fast), and do not, must redeem their neglect by the maintenance of one poor man " (' Koran,' chap. ii.) Under the Christian Emperor Charlemagne, on the contrary, and even so late as the 17th century, the breaking of the Christian fast was punished with death by decapitation, as appears from a sentence passed by the Chief Judge of the Saint Claude Jurisdiction, upon one Claude Guillon, convicted of having eaten, on the 1st April, 1629, some pieces of a horse which had been killed and left in a meadow ; a sentence that was duly executed on the 28th of the following July. On which side, it may be asked, were humanity and civilization ?

opposed the nascent religion in every way; plots for the Prophet's assassination were continually being concocted, but were all defeated by his imperturbable coolness and incessant vigilance. So great was now Mohammed's influence that he succeeded in abolishing the use of wine, causing the juice of the grape to be held in abhorrence by all true Mussulmans. This moral ascendency was indispensably necessary in order to save Islam from succumbing under the assaults of the numerous and bitter enemies by which it was surrounded. In fact the Koreish had now united themselves with the Jews; many Arabian tribes also arrived from their deserts, and all these forces making common cause together, advanced against Medina, where Islam awaited them with no other support than the determined will of a man of genius, an inextinguishable enthusiasm, and an invincible constancy and devotedness. All the efforts of the besiegers failed. After every sortie Mohammed re-entered Medina triumphant, and the siege being at length raised, Mohammed directed his army against the tribe of the Coraids and, in a pitched battle, defeated them utterly.

It is necessary to notice here, with a view to refutation, a malicious charge brought, about this time, against Mohammed, by his enemies—that of having committed incest by marrying the divorced wife of his adopted son. The real facts are these: long before the promulgation of Islam, it was a custom among the Arabs that if any person happened to call his wife—mother, he could no longer continue to cohabit with her; or should he call any youth—son, the latter would thenceforth be entitled to all the rights of a real one. Now, both these customs having been abolished by the Koran, a man might therefore still continue to live with his wife, even after he had called her mother, or could marry the wife of his adopted son upon her being divorced. Mohammed having a great esteem for a maiden named Zaïnab, proposed her marriage with Zeid, a youth for whom also he had a like esteem. The marriage not proving a happy one, Zeid determined upon a divorce, notwithstanding all the remonstrances of Mohammed. The latter, conscious that he himself was to blame in having originally recommended the marriage, and moved by the tears and distress of Zaïnab, resolved to make her the only reparation in his power, that of marrying her himself after her divorce from Zeid. It was with difficulty he determined upon this step, being apprehensive that such of his countrymen who still retained the custom above mentioned would accuse him of incest, but a strong sense of duty overcame these objections, and Zaïnab became the wife of the Prophet.

At the close of a successful expedition against the tribes, Ayesha, so dearly beloved of the Prophet, was accused of having been guilty of adultery with a young officer by name Sawa, but her artless and unreserved explanation, aided by the irresistible eloquence of tears and beauty, sufficed to convince Mohammed of her innocence, and her accusers were punished by receiving, severally, eighty stripes.

The Jews dwelling in the neighbourhood of Mula Medina having been attacked and severely treated by Mohammed, applied to the Meccans for aid, and having received a strong auxiliary force, marched against Medina. Mohammed, whom the defeat at Ahed had rendered cautious, having, by the advice of a Persian convert, dug a moat round the city for its defence, allowed the enemy to pillage the open country, after which they proceeded to lay siege to the city, but being repulsed in several attempts to storm it, and dissentions also arising among them, they broke up their encampment and returned home. This war, called "the war of the *Moat*," took place A.D. 625-26, being the fourth year of the Hegira. Mohammed now assumed the offensive, seizing the fortresses of Nacon and Elocoab, and after a fierce and obstinate resistance, that of Khaïbar, which last town he entered little aware of the danger there awaiting him, and which was as follows :—A young Jewess who had lost her father, her husband, her brother and other relatives in the late battles, impelled by a spirit of revenge, determined to destroy Mohammed as the enemy of her race and family. Having, therefore, dressed a kid, and steeped it in a deadly poison, she placed it, with fair words, before the Prophet at the hour of his evening repast. Scarcely had he swallowed the first mouthful, than he cried out, "Hold; surely this kid has been poisoned!" Bisr, one of his officers, who had eaten more than Mohammed, at once turned pale, moving neither hand nor foot, until he died. Mohammed, who was also seized with excruciating pains, immediately caused himself and all those who like himself had partaken of the dish, to be freely cupped between the shoulders. The young Jewess being summoned and inter-rogated, boldly replied, "Thou, Mohammed, slewedst my father, husband and brother, therefore, I said to myself, 'if he be a real prophet, he will be aware that the kid is poi-soned, but if he be a mere pretender then shall we be rid of him and the Jews will once more prosper!'" She was instantly put to death. The prophet was ill for a long time after, and as he never completely recovered from the effects of the poison, it is by no means surprising that the vengeance he took upon the Jews was so terrible that many of their towns, struck with fear, submitted, uncondition-ally, the Prophet's power being thereby still more firmly established. Allies, also, from all quarters, offered them-selves, their conversion having, in many cases, been effected by the profound impression which the reading of the Koran produced upon their minds.

To visit that ancient and hallowed Kaaba, to which, when reciting his daily prayers, he turned his reverential gaze, had long been the pious and devout wish of every true Mussulman, a desire which Mohammed encouraged to the utmost, impelled as he himself was by the hope of conquering and converting Mecca, and of entering as a victorious monarch a city where he had formerly been subjected to so many insults and exposed to such great dangers. He therefore lost no time in placing himself at the head of all the faithful for the purpose of undertaking what he called a peaceful pilgrimage to the Kaaba, and, although he met with opposition at almost every step, nevertheless, he and his thousand followers advanced victoriously towards the city. Islam, moreover, had already within the walls its secret partisans, and the terror inspired by the very name of Mohammed, added to the marvels said to have accompanied his mission, all contributed to induce the Koreish to be the first to propose terms of accommodation, which ended in a treaty between themselves and the Mohammedans, the conditions of the treaty being :—

1. A truce of three years shall be faithfully observed, and kept between the contracting parties.

2. The Arab tribes shall be at liberty to take part either with Mohammed or with the Meccans.

3. Mohammed and his followers shall quit the sacred territory within the present year.

4. The Mohammedans may, during this year, visit the holy places known as the Eleeda.

5. The Mohammedans shall enter Mecca with no other arms than their sheathed swords.

6. They shall sojourn therein three days, and shall not compel any citizen to quit it against his will.

The above treaty was the greatest success hitherto achieved by Mohammed, for although the Prophet himself might return to Medina after having duly performed the ceremonies enjoined by the Koran, Islamism still remained firmly established there, and the power of each of the 360 idols* was sapped to its very foundation as soon as the Prophet, standing erect beside the Black Stone, in the Kaaba, proclaimed aloud the name of the true God.

* The ancient year of the Arabians contained 360 days, each of which had its idol. These idols represented men, eagles, lions and antelopes, among which stood conspicuous the most popular of them, the statue of Hobal, fashioned of red agate by a Syrian artist, and holding in his hand seven arrows without heads or feathers, the instruments and symbols of profane divination.

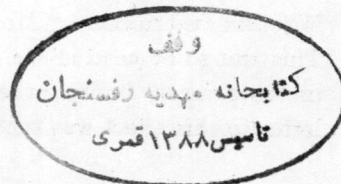

CHAPTER III.

Embassies from princes to the Prophet—King of Abyssinia's letter—The
  Prophet's seal—Letter to the King of Persia, who insults the Prophet—
  Mohammed's denunciation of him—Expedition against Besra—Merciful
  injunctions of the Prophet—Heroic deaths of Zeid, Jauffer and Abdoollah
  —Khaled the "Sword of God"—The Koreish violate the treaty—Expe-
  dition against Mecca—The city surrenders at discretion—Idols demo-
  lished by Mohammed's own hand—His clemency to the conquered—
  Restitution of spoil—Proposal of Moseilama, Prince of Yemen—The
  Prophet's indignant reply—Idolatry extirpated throughout Arabia—
  Successful expedition against Syria—Death of the Prophet's only son—
  Eclipse of the sun—Mohammed rebukes the superstition of his followers
  —Particulars of Mohammed's death—Story respecting his coffin refuted
  —The number of the *Beast*, 666, applied to Mohammed—Thos. Carlyle's
  view of Mohammed's character—The vastness of the Empire founded by
  him, and rapid progress of his religion—Christian relics replaced by
  Mohammedan ones—Omar in the Church of St. Sophia (note).

IN the ninth year of the Hegira embassies arrived at Mecca
and Medina from all parts to tender the submission of various
princes to the Prophet. The king of Abyssinia, to whom
Mohammed had despatched a special messenger, replied,
" Peace be to God, the Holy King, the faithful, true,
powerful and mighty Saviour ! I attest that there is but
one God, and that Mohammed is his prophet. The Apostle
of God hath written to me to ask, in marriage, my
daughter, Omome Hababa. I joyfully fulfil his wish, and
give, as her dower, 4,000 gold crowns."

About this time, also, Mohammed had a seal made, bearing this inscription, " Mohammed, the Apostle of God."
This was to be used in sealing the letters written by him to
divers princes, inviting them to embrace Islam. His first
letter to this effect was sent to Badham, Viceroy of Yemen,

to be forwarded to Khosroes, King of Persia. Khosroes tore the letter in pieces, ordering Badham either to restore the Prophet to his right mind, or to send him his head. As soon as this insult was made known to the Prophet, he exclaimed, "Thus shall Allah tear asunder the kingdom of Khosroes, and reject his supplications." Khosroes was soon after murdered by his son Sirses. Badham, with his people became Mussulmans, and Mohammed continued him in his government. Herodius, the Roman Emperor, who, as Arab historians assure us, received an epistle addressed to him by Mohammed, with the utmost respect, placing it under his pillow, despatched an embassy to the Prophet, with rich presents. Two other sovereigns, Hawansa and Elmonda had come, of their own accord, to visit Mohammed, and embrace Islam at his feet. Such success is easily accounted for by the fact that in Mohammed was to be found united, not only great elevation of character and a mighty power of the sword, but also a rich persuasive eloquence, so that words falling from his lips having all the force of inspiration, made the deepest impression upon the imagination of the Arabs, and being repeated from mouth to mouth, reached the remotest parts. The *Book*, also, which Mohammed offered to them and to the whole Eastern world, was full of magnificent promises ; a book, moreover, which exacted little but rewarded much, and whence emanated an irresistible authority attracting everything to itself.

While establishing a sovereignty at Mecca and Medina, the Prophet had endeavoured to extend the revolution to the people and princes of the adjacent countries ; but the messenger to the Governor of Bossa, near Damascus, was taken prisoner and murdered by Sherheil, an emir of a Christian and Arabian tribe, tributary to Heraclius, the Greek emperor. The injury was trifling, but the insult was great. Three thousand men were immediately equipped ; the Prophet exhorted them to display their courage in the cause of the Most High, and painted to them, in glowing colours, the joys of an earthly and heavenly paradise, the reward of such Moslems who were victorious or were slain. At the same time, however, he enjoined them to collect their booty not from the tears of the provincials, but from the public treasuries of the conquered state : " In avenging my injuries," said he, "molest not the harmless votaries of domestic seclusion; spare the weakness of the softer sex, the infant at the breast, and those who, in the course of nature, are hastening from this scene of mortality. Abstain from demolishing the dwellings of the unresisting inhabitants, and destroy not the means of subsistence; respect their fruit trees, nor injure the palm, so useful to Syria for its shade and so delightful for its verdure."*

The Greeks being vastly superior in number (for, including the auxiliary Arabs, they had an army of about a hundred thousand men), the Moslems were repulsed in the first attack, and lost successively three of their generals, Zeid, Jauffer and Abdoollah, appointed by Mohammed to replace each other in case of loss. Zeid fell like a soldier in the foremost ranks. The death of Jauffer was heroic and memorable ; his right hand being severed from the arm, he shifted the standard to his left, and upon losing this his remaining hand, he embraced the sacred banner with his bleeding stumps until transfixed with fifty honourable wounds. Abdoollah, filling up the vacant place, cried aloud, "Forward; and victory or Paradise is our own !" A Greek lance determined the alternative, but the falling standard was seized by Khaled, a new proselyte ; nine swords were broken in his hand, and his valour withstood and repulsed the almost overwhelming forces of the Christians. Victory at length declared itself for the Moslems, and Khaled, whose skill and intrepidity had so greatly contributed to

---

* " Revere," says the Koran, "your aunt, the palm tree ; for it is made of the remainder of the clay of which Adam was formed."

insure it had, as a reward, the honourable title of "The sword of God," conferred upon him by Mohammed.

The Koreish had broken the treaty entered into, as above narrated, by affording aid to the enemies of Mohammed, and it therefore became necessary to reduce them to subjection. After making the requisite preparations, Mohammed left Medina at the head of ten thousand men ; but the success of the expedition was nearly compromised by private treachery. Sarah, a female servant had been sent by her master, Haleb, to convey a letter to the Meccans, in which he informed them of the danger that threatened them, but Ali having learnt the circumstance just in time, mounting his horse, pursued and overtook the messenger. She stoutly denied having any letter about her, nor, upon searching her was it to be found. Ali, enraged at being thus baffled, drew his scimitar, and was brandishing it over the girl's head, when, trembling with terror, she loosened her long tresses, from which fell a letter containing these words :—" Haleb, son of Batten, to the Meccans—health ! The apostle of God is preparing to attack you ! To arms !"

Such was the celerity of Mohammed's movements that he was at the gates of Mecca before the Koreish had any idea of his approach. The city surrendered at discretion, and Mohammed, clad in a scarlet robe and mounted on his favourite camel, Al Kaswa, entered it in triumph. Abu Sophian being brought before him, purchased life upon the condition of embracing Islam. Mohammed next proceeded to demolish, with his own hand, the idols in the temple, and having ridden seven times round the Kaaba, promulgated the sacred formula, "There is but one God, and Mohammed is his prophet !" He then went to quench his thirst at the well of Zamzam, the same which the angel had shown to Hagar in the wilderness, after which he read to the assembled people the 48th chapter of the

Koran.* Then, when he heard the Muezin for the first time call the people to prayers, when the fragments of the broken idols had been removed, and all the multitude pressed around him: "What," said he, "do you ask of me?" "That you treat us as a father," replied a thousand suppliant voices. "Go," was the answer, "go; and may the blessing of Allah rest upon you!"

In the meantime the Havazen and Koreish tribes commanded by Abalak, being deeply incensed at seeing their sacred idols demolished, took up arms and appeared in battle array in the valley of Honain, about three miles from Mecca. Twelve thousand men, including two thousand Meccans, recently converted, promised themselves an easy victory over those tribes so inferior in numbers; but, being unexpectedly assailed with a storm of darts, the Mussulman army, terrified by so sudden an attack, was about to make a disgraceful retreat. Under such circumstances something more was necessary than to invoke the name of Allah, or call for angelic aid. The active arm, as well as the directing head was required. Mohammed, therefore, rushed into the thickest of the fight, and by his personal intrepidity and valour arrested the flight of his troops, and ultimately defeated his foe. After a long and vigorous pursuit, the Havazens tendered their submission, and Abalak set the example to his people of embracing the new faith. Six thousand prisoners, twenty-four thousand horses, four thousand mouhars, and the like number of ounces of silver, fell into the victor's hands. The division of this rich spoil was

* "VERILY, We (God) have won for thee (Mohammed) a manifest VICTORY—

"In token that God forgiveth thy earlier and later sins, and fulfilleth His goodness to thee, and guideth thee on the right way,

"And that God succoureth thee with a mighty succour.

"He it is who sendeth down a spirit of secure repose into the hearts of the faithful that they might add faith to their faith (for God's are the armies of the heavens and of the earth); and God is knowing and wise," etc., etc.

about to be made when deputies arrived who, with tears and lamentations, besought Mohammed not to ruin so many families ; upon which the Prophet assembling his soldiers addressed to them these few and simple words.— "Mussulmans, your brethren have come to you led by repentance ! They have besought me to give freedom to their fathers, mothers and children, and restore to them their property and effects. I could not resist their prayer. Your approval will afford me heartfelt satisfaction ; but, should any one think himself injured thereby, let him speak, and I will promise to indemnify him at the next battle, when Allah shall vouchsafe unto us still richer spoils." Not a murmur was heard when Mohammed finished his appeal ; everything taken was restored, all the captives were set at liberty, and the spirit of religion and justice replaced that of violence and rapine.

Among the Arab princes who now came in crowds to make profession of Islam was Moseilama, Prince of Yemen. This personage, who was nothing better than an ambitious hypocrite, on returning to his dominions, was tempted by Mohammed's success, and forgetting that genius and conviction were essential for enacting the part of prophet, apostatized and wrote thus to Mohammed :—" Moseilama, the Apostle of God, to Mohammed, the Apostle of God ! Let one half of the world be mine, and the other half thine."

Mohammed answered thus :—" Mohammed, the Apostle of God, to Moseilama, the liar. The earth belongeth to God, who giveth the inheritance thereof to whom it pleaseth him."

In the tenth year of the Hegira, Ali was sent into Yemen, there to popagate the faith of Islam, and it is said that the whole tribe of Hemden were converted in one day, an example quickly followed by all the inhabitants of that province, with the exception only of those of Nejram, who being Christians, preferred paying tribute.

Thus was Islam established and idolatry rooted out, in Mohammed's lifetime (for he died the very next year), throughout Arabia; nor was this success attributable to his warlike genius alone, but also to his being a reformer as well as a conqueror, to the religion which he promulgated being that of the patriarchs of old, and, lastly, to his system of morality which, however it may appear to modern Christians, was purity itself when compared with the contemporary practice of Arabia. Add to this, that his law which prohibited retaliation, without the previous sanction of a trial and a judicial sentence, was a bold and laudable attempt to bridle the vindictive passions of his countrymen, so long fostered by the practice of private war, and for that very reason materially conduced to the same end.

The conversion of the Arabs, therefore, was probably as sincere as it was general; and their religious spirit being now thoroughly aroused, every feeling of their enthusiastic nature was turned into one channel: to conquer in the cause of God, or to die in asserting his unity and greatness, was the ardent and ever-present wish of every Mussulman; the love of power or of spoil, the thirst for glory, and even the hopes of Paradise, only contributed to swell the tide of this absorbing passion.

The whole of Arabia being, as above said, purified from idolatry and acknowledging Mohammed's formula—" There is but one God, and Mohammed is His prophet!"—this religious conqueror turned his anxious thoughts to the subjugation of Syria, with the view of wresting that country from the Greeks and establishing Islam therein; a project which he publicly announced in the year A.D. 639. No time was to be lost in executing his intention. A long campaign was to be commenced when the fruits were ripening, the harvests were ready, and when the sun heated still more intensely the burning sands of Arabia. It was now that a more implicit obedience than ever was paid to a will the

more powerful because believed to have come from God.
Twenty thousand infantry and ten thousand cavalry, all well
armed and appointed, set forth under the command of
Mohammed, from the peaceful walls of the city of Medina.
But the obstacles and dangers of the march surpassed even
the most sinister forebodings. After hitherto unheard of
sufferings and privations, the expedition at length reached
Syria, where scarcely any opposition was encountered,
for, after a few skirmishes, all the petty princes among
whom that country was then divided, came into the Mussulman camp and prostrated themselves at the feet of the
Prophet, the fame of whose exploits sufficed to vanquish
them. Mohammed imposed tribute and exacted ransoms,
but in every instance respected the religious belief of the
conquered, always, it is true, recommending his religion,
but never enforcing its adoption by law ; thus carrying into
execution what he had written in the Koran, "Say unto
the blind (in spirit), 'Embrace Islam, and you shall be
enlightened.' " "If they are rebels, you are only charged
with preaching unto them ; God knoweth how to distinguish his servants !"*

Mohammed's success in this instance principally arose
from the clemency and moderation he showed to the Christians, from whom he claimed only a moderate tribute. Thus,
when he returned to Medina, he left in the country he had
subjected every heart astonished at the clemency of his
religion.

About this period of Mohammed's history, an event
occurred which, in the opinion of every candid and impar-
tial mind, exonerates him from all the imputations of
imposture with which he has been assailed. His only son,
Ibrahim, whom he had by Mariyeh, a Coptic slave-girl,
when he was sixty-one years of age, had just died when
seventeen years old. It was, indeed, an agonizing loss for

* See chapters ii., xlv., and lxxxviii.

the father thus to see extinguished in him the only one who
could transmit to posterity so illustrious a name. An
eclipse of the sun occurring precisely at the very hour of
the youth's decease, the common people saw in this prodigy
a sure token that the heavens themselves shared the general
grief; but so far from encouraging this superstitious feeling
on the part of his ignorant followers—so far from listening
to the voice of flattery—Mohammed called the people
together, and said to them : " Fellow citizens, the sun and
the stars are the works of God's hands, but they are neither
eclipsed nor effaced to announce the birth or the death of
mortals."* From this time, Mohammed was chiefly occupied
in receiving the homage of all who came to Medina to
reverence the Koran, and in enacting the laws and establishing the institutions of that empire which was destined
to extend itself over one half, and that, the fairest portion, of
the globe. Wishing, by a striking example, to impress
upon the minds of the people a due regard and respect for
the external rites of his religion, he caused it to be everywhere announced that he intended performing a pilgrimage
to Mecca, and, as if he had had some presentiment that it
would be his last one, the Prophet was careful to make it
the most splendid ceremonial that had ever been witnessed
in that city. A brief outline of the forms he observed upon
this occasion is here given, they being the rules by which
pilgrims to Mecca are guided even in the present day.
Having performed the prescribed ablutions and shaved his
head, Mohammed proceeded to the Temple, kissed the Black
Stone, made seven times the circuit of the Kaaba, then
leaving the city, he walked with slow and solemn steps to
the hill of Sufa, and turning himself in the direction of the

---

* This privation of male issue was a never-ceasing source of regret,
humiliation, and mortification to Mohammed; inasmuch as those who were
envious of his success gave him the nickname of *Abdar* (one whose tail has
been cut off)—that is to say, *childless.*

Kaaba, exclaimed with a loud voice, "God is great : there is no God but God ! He hath no companions ; to Him alone belong might, majesty and power ! Praised be His holy name ! There is no God but God !"—Leaving Sufa, he repeated the same formula at Merva and the other sacred stations : lastly, he sacrificed sixty-three camels, one for each year of his life, and liberated the like number of slaves.

Mohammed now returned to Medina, where death awaited him, in the midst of all the mighty projects still meditated by that inexhaustible genius. Shortly after his arrival he was attacked by a bilious fever, and believing that it would prove dangerous, if not fatal, he was desirous of being surrounded by those whom he most dearly loved. He chose as his dying place the apartments of his favourite wife, Ayesha. His agony was long and painful, and, during the paroxysms, he often cried out : " It is the Jewish poison that is killing me ; I feel every vein in my heart cracking !" He retained, notwithstanding, the full possession of his faculties, so much so, indeed, that he arranged all the details of another expedition into Syria, blessed the standard of Islam, and entrusted it to the zeal, fidelity and valour of Omar, who was to command the troops. Till the third day before his death, he regularly performed the ceremonies of public worship ; but when he was so ill as to enter the mosque resting on the shoulders of his servants, his feet dragging after him, he ordered his ancient and faithful friend Abu-Bekr to read the service. On the last time of his attendance, and on the conclusion of the prayers, he edified all present by the humility and sincerity of his penitence, in thus addressing them :—" Men and brethren, if I have caused any one of you to be unjustly scourged, I here submit my own shoulders to the lash of retaliation. Have I aspersed the good name of any Mussulman ? let him proclaim my faults before this congregation ! Has any one been despoiled of his goods ? the little that I have shall discharge the debt, both principal and interest!" One present claiming an old debt of three drachmas, Mohammed immediately caused him to be paid, saying, "I would rather blush in this world than in that which is to come!" His daughter Fatima came frequently to sit by his dying bed: "Daughter," said he to her, "wherefore weepest thou? art thou not satisfied with being, both on earth and in heaven, the chiefest among women?" He then gave liberty to his slaves. To his other relatives, who, bathed in tears, surrounded his couch, he said, "I shall now instruct you what you are to do after my decease. Having washed my corpse, wrapped it in the shroud, and laid it in the coffin, you will rest it on the edge of the grave, which must be dug beneath the spot where I now am; these duties fulfilled, you will then depart." After a pause, he continued: "The first who will come to pray for me will be my faithful friend Gabriel, followed by Asraphael and Michael, and after them, the Angel of Death accompanied by his legions. Upon their departure you may enter, in groups, to pray for me and implore for me the peace of heaven. My family must put on mourning, thus setting an example to be followed by all the faithful. My most earnest wish and desire are that no wailings or lamentations disturb my repose." Mohammed now became, for a few moments, unconscious, but having recovered, said, "I will dictate a book which shall prevent your ever backsliding into error;" on which, Omar holding up the Koran, immediately exclaimed, "The book is written!" After this all quitted the room, his beloved Ayesha only excepted. On the day of his decease he bathed his hands in water, crying out, "O God! fortify my soul against the terrors of death!" Soon after he became faint. "The moment of his agony," says Ayesha, "was come. I was seated by his side, his head reclining on my lap. Suddenly opening his eyes, he raised them towards the roof of the house, and with a steadfast look, but faltering voice, uttered these last broken, although articulate words, 'O God, pardon my sins! Ah, my companion (Gabriel), I attend thee to the realms above,' and he then peacefully expired on a carpet spread on the floor."

Mohammed died on the 13th Raby, the first day of the eleventh year of the Hegira, and answering to the 8th of June, 632 A.D., at the age of sixty-three, during the last twenty-seven of which he had assumed the character of a prophet. He was buried at Medina, not at Mecca; his coffin is not suspended in the air by the attraction of loadstones of equal power, as has been so ridiculously asserted,* but is deposited in the ground, to the right of those of Abu-Bekr and Omar.†

Mohammed's death produced a general consternation; the question was everywhere asked, " Can the religion survive him, seeing that the living letter is dead?" Omar replied that the Prophet could not perish. "As in the cases of Moses and Jesus Christ," said he, "his soul has disappeared for an instant, but it will return into the midst of the faithful." It required all the authority of Abu-Bekr to combat the opinion, which Omar was ready to maintain at the sword's point. "Is it of Mohammed or of God that you speak, O Omar? The God of Mohammed is immortal; but Mohammed was a man like unto one of us, and perished as we ourselves shall." Abu-Bekr had still some difficulty in allaying the tumult, but at length succeeded by reading

---

* The idea was, no doubt, taken from Pliny the Elder, who states ('Hist. Natur.,' lib. xxxiv. 42) that Dinocrates, the Greek architect, who rebuilt the famous temple of Ephesus, which had been destroyed by Erostrates, had begun to roof the temple of Arsinoe at Alexandria, with loadstones, in order that the image of that queen, which was made of iron, might appear to hang in the air.

† The Mohammedans believe that Jesus Christ will return to earth at the end of the world; that he will slay the Anti-Christ, die, and be raised again. A vacant place is reserved for Christ's body in Mohammed's tomb at Medina. (See Lieut. Burton's ' Pilgrimage,' vol. ii.)

those passages of the Koran wherein the prophet himself asserted his mortality.

The four immediate successors of Mohammed were Abu-Bekr, Omar, Othman and Ali, who all reigned under the title of Caliph.*

It may here be remarked that the sword which had been so irresistible in the hand of Mohammed was never sheathed by his successors till it had established a vast empire, comprising extensive portions of Asia, Africa, and Europe. Under the banners of Omar, Khaled, and other chief captains of Mohammed, victory followed victory. Persia, Palestine, Syria, and Egypt submitted in rapid succession to their Saracenic invaders. In twelve years they reduced to obedience thirty-six thousand cities, towns or castles; destroyed four thousand temples or churches; and built fourteen hundred mosques dedicated to the religion of their founder; nor did they stay their progress until they had subjugated the Moors, and brought all Africa, from Alexandria to Tangiers, together with the greatest part of Spain, under their lordly sway.

On the graces and intellectual gifts of nature to the son of Abdoollah, the Arabian writers dwell with the proudest and fondest satisfaction. His politeness to the great, his affability to the humble, and his dignified bearing to the presumptuous, procured him respect, admiration and applause. His talents were equally fitted for persuasion or command. Deeply read in the volume of nature, though entirely ignorant of letters, his mind could expand into controversy with the acutest of his enemies, or contract itself to the apprehension of the meanest of his disciples. His simple eloquence, rendered impressive by the expression of a countenance wherein awfulness of majesty was tempered

---

* Our biographical memoir naturally and properly terminating with the Prophet's death, the reader is referred to the controversial writers, for an account of the disputes between the Soonites and the Sheahs respecting the succession to the Caliphate.

by an amiable sweetness, excited emotions of veneration and love; and he was gifted with that authoritative air of genius which alike influences the learned and commands the illiterate. As a friend and a parent, he exhibited the softest feelings of our nature ;* but, while in possession of the kind and generous emotions of the heart, and engaged in the discharge of most of the social and domestic duties, he disgraced not his assumed title of an apostle of God. With all that simplicity which is so natural to a great mind, he performed the humbler offices whose homeliness it would be idle to conceal with pompous diction; even while Lord of Arabia, he mended his own shoes and coarse woollen garments, milked the ewes, swept the hearth, and kindled the fire. Dates and water were his usual fare, and milk and honey his luxuries. When he travelled he divided his morsel with his servant. The sincerity of his exhortations to benevolence were justified at his death by the exhausted state of his coffers.†

The view taken by Thomas Carlyle of this hero-prophet is too original, just and striking to be here omitted :—" The deep-hearted son of the wilderness," writes he, "with his beaming black eyes, and open, social, deep soul, had other thoughts in him than ambition. A silent, great soul; he was one of those who cannot but be in earnest; whom

* Upon the death of Zeid, who was killed at the battle of Mutah, one of Mohammed's disciples surprised him weeping in his chamber with the daughter of that faithful servant and friend. "What do I see ?" exclaimed the intruder, astonished that the weakness of humanity should dwell in the breast of an apostle from heaven. "You see," replied the Prophet "one who is deploring the loss of a beloved and devoted friend." Mohammed's affection for Fatima, his daughter by Khadijah, was of unbounded tenderness, and when he followed his other children to an untimely grave, he wept in all the agony that can rend the fond heart of a parent.

† The more insight is obtained from undoubted historical sources as to the real character of Mohammed, the less reason will there be found to justify the strong and vituperative language poured upon his head by Maracci, Prideaux, and more recently by Frederick Schlegel and others, one

Nature herself has appointed to be sincere. While others walk in formulas and hearsays, contented enough to dwell therein, this man could not screen himself in formulas : he was alone with his own soul and the reality of things. The great mystery of existence glared in upon him, with its terrors, with its splendours; no hearsays could hide that unspeakable fact, 'Here am I!' Such *sincerity* as we named, it has, in truth, something of divine. The word of such a man is a voice direct from Nature's own heart. Men do and must listen to that, or to nothing else; all else is wind in comparison. From of old, a thousand thoughts in his pilgrimages and wanderings had been in this man. 'What am I? What is this unfathomable Thing I live in, which men name Universe? What is Life? What is Death? What am I to believe? What am I to do?' The grim rocks of Mount Hara, of Mount Sinai, the stern sandy solitudes answered not. The great heaven rolling silently overhead with its blue glancing stars, answered not. There was no answer. The man's own soul, and what of God's inspiration dwelt there, had to answer !"*

Mohammed, a private man, made himself to be looked upon as a prophet by his own family. Mohammed, a simple Arab, united the distracted, scanty, naked and hungry tribes of his country into one compact and obedient body, and presented them with new attributes and a new character among the people of the earth. In less than thirty years

---

of whom has even pretended to find in the Byzantine *Maomeths* the number of the *Beast* (Rev. xii.) thus : —

M	40
A	1
O	70
M	40
E	5
T	300
H	10
S	200

Number of the *Beast* 666

* Carlyle's Works, vol. vi. p. 225.

this system defeated the Emperor of Constantinople, over-
threw the Kings of Persia; subdued Syria, Mesopotamia,
Egypt; and extended its conquests from the Atlantic to the
Caspian Ocean, and to the Oxus; from which limits, during
twelve centuries, its political sway has never, with the exception of Spain only, receded; while the faith has continued
to extend, and is, at this hour, extending in Northern Asia,
in Central Africa, and on the Caspian.

Such was Mohammed, the hero-prophet, whose enthusiasm
and genius founded a religion which was to reduce the followers of Zoroaster to a few scattered communities, to invade
India, to overpower the ancient Brahmanism, as well as the
more wide-spread Buddhism even beyond the Ganges; to
wrest her most ancient and venerable provinces from
Christianity, to subjugate by degrees the whole of her
Eastern dominions and Roman Africa, from Egypt to the
Straits of Gibraltar, to assail Europe at its western extre-
mity, to possess the greater part of Spain, and to advance
to the borders of the Loire, which was to make the elder
Rome tremble for her security, and, finally, to establish
itself in triumph, within the new Rome of Constantinople.*

---

* Among the relics, Constantinople still preserves Mohammed's cloak
(*burda*), and black banner called *Okab* (black eagle); these replaced in the
church of St. Sophia (the Christian Church of the Lower Empire, changed
into a mosque), the remains and the nails of the true Cross on which Jesus
Christ was crucified; and which relics had been brought from Jerusalem
by the mother of Constantine the Great. It was in this same church of
St. Sophia, on one of its pillars, that a mark appears made by Omar, who,
riding his war-horse into the church, on the heaped-up bodies of the
Christians slain, dashed the marble with his bloody hand to show, as it were,
the high-water mark of God's indignation against a perverse generation,
which, having had the truth delivered to it, fell away to weakness, wickedness, folly and lust.

Translation of an Arabic poem entitled the ' BORDA,' written in praise of Mohammed by Sharf-ood-din Al-Basari.

Mohammed is the Prince of both the worlds,
   That of men and that of Genii.
Sovereign, likewise, is he of the two worlds
   Of Arabians and of barbarians.
He is our Prophet, who unto us prescribeth
   What we should do and what we should avoid.
Of all men Mohammed the most truthful is,
   Whether he affirm or whether he deny ;
He is the friend of God ; his intercession it is
   On which alone our every hope is based ;
And in him alone a defence is to be sought
   Against the most appalling of dangers.
It is he that hath called the sons of men
   To know the true, the only God ;
   Whosoever shall lay fast hold upon him
   Graspeth a cable that will not part asunder.
All other prophets Mohammed hath surpassed
    By the excellence of his external qualities,
      By his moral and intellectual gifts.
In virtue and in knowledge none approacheth him.
   From God's apostle every soul soliciteth
One draught from out the ocean of his knowledge,
   One drop of the copious showers of his virtues.
   Near Mohammed each filleth the rank befitting him,
    For as a point or accent is to the written word,
So are their knowledge and virtue in comparison of his.
He it is who is alike perfect and estimable
   By the qualities and graces of the heart and person.
The Creator of the soul selected him for friend ;
   No earthly being can aspire to share with him
    His incomparable and boundless virtues.

His alone is the substance of excellence itself.
Let the dignity of their prophet be, of Christians,
   The profane and fallacious boast;
But do thou, excepting only the Divine essence,
   Sing, unrestricted, the praises of the Prophet!
Extol to the utmost the excellence of his valour;
   Applaud to the full the eminence of his merits;
For the excellence of God's apostle is boundless;
   Nor are there words wherewithal to set it forth;
Vainly would men strive to comprehend
   The excellence of his mental endowments,
Just as when seen from far, of day's bright orb
   The enormous magnitude is not apparent,
But dazzles and confounds the vision
   Of him who near beholds it.
How can mortals, plunged in oblivious sleep,
   And contented with imagination's idle dreams,
Attain, in this world, to the perfect ken
   Of what God's prophet truly is?
That he is a man, and of all God's creatures
   The most excellent, is all of him we know.
How worthy of admiration is the prophet's face,
   Of which the charms by virtues are enhanced!
In him is centred every captivating grace;
   But for his real, and distinctive character
Are features beaming with amiability and candour.
Verily, in his person he doth unite
   The delicate beauty of the flower of spring
     With the majestic grandeur of the moon.
Vast as the sea is his generosity, his designs
   As time itself, extensive and enduring.
Such is the majesty of the Prophet's countenance,
   That even when alone his presence is
   Unto every beholder as redoubtable
   As when at the head of mighty armies,
   Or in the midst of conquering cohorts.

The fragrance of the earth which covereth his bones
    Surpasseth far the richest perfumes.
Happy, thrice happy, those who inhale that fragrance,
    And who moisten the soil with their kisses !
Now let me hymn the Prophet's holy oracles.
As in some lofty mountain shines from far,
    Amid the darkness of the moonless night,
A fire beacon lighted by some kindly hand
    To lead the traveller to some friendly hearth,
So do those oracles irradiate with their beams
    The gloom and darkness of a sinful world.
From mercy's God did come those oracles divine ;
    In time truly have they been produced ;
But born of Him whose essence is eternal,
    Therefore themselves, eternal are ;
Neither can any mortal epoch be to them assigned,
From them we learn what on the last tremendous day,
    The day of retributive justice,
Shall come to pass ; from them we learn
    What happen'd in the days of Ad and Iran.
    O thou who enjoyest this happiness supreme,
Rejoice ! for thou hast seized the cable
Which is the Almighty—God himself !
Beware permitting it to escape thy grasp !
Shouldest thou therein read, to find a refuge
Safe from Hell's scorching heat,
    The refreshing waters of the Book divine
    Will cool the ardours of th' infernal pit.
Straight as is the bridge of Sirah,
Just as is the balance wherein are weighed
    The deeds of all who live.
These oracles are the sole, the only source
    Of right and justice among the sons of men.
Marvel not their worth should be denied
    By envious men, who act in this as if insane,
Although possessed of knowledge and discernment.

Seest thou not that to the eye bedimmed with age
    The brightness of day's orb seems overcast ;
And that the palate of him who's sick
    Appreciates not the flavour of the clear, pellucid stream.
O thou most excellent of all created beings !
To whom but thee can I flee for refuge
    In that moment so terrible to every mortal ?
O, Apostle of God ! thy glory will not be tarnished
    By whatsoever aid thou may'st vouchsafe me
In that tremendous day wherein the Almighty
    Himself shall manifest as the Avenger !
Verily this world, as well as that which is to come.
    Are the wondrous works of his beneficence !
And every decree traced by the eternal pen
    Upon the tablets of the Most High,
Form part of thy transcendant knowledge !

PART II.

THE KORAN.

THE KORAN.[*]

CHAPTER I.

Derivation of the word *Koran*—Other appellations given to it—Editions of
(note)—Is the miracle of Mohammed—The table of God's decrees and
the Kullum—Revelation of the Koran to Mohammed—Metrical account
of the 6666 verses of the Koran—The Koran the most poetical work of
the East—Göthe's opinion of it—How it was preserved—Conversion of
the poet Lebid—Reverence of Mohammedans for the Koran—The Koran
a code of laws—Differs materially from the Bible—Mistrust of priests
both by Jesus Christ and Mohammed (Renan quoted)—Mohammedan
idea of the Deity—Hindoo definition of the divinity—Mohammed's high
and mysterious respect for Jesus Christ—The Immaculate Conception
borrowed from the Koran—Celebrated text of the "three witnesses"—
The Trinity (note)—Belief of Christ's return to the earth—Place for him
in Mohammed's tomb—General design of the Koran—Analysis of it—
Moslem conquerors and Roman pontiffs compared—M. Jurieu quoted—
Exclusive character of Judaism—The four Gospels (note)—Christian
Church in Constantine's time—Intellectual image of the Deity never
disgraced by any visible idol—Propagation of Islam by the sword, a
monstrous error—Mohammedanism ordained for much eventual good.

THE word Koran is derived from the Arabic Koraä (he
read), and properly signifies "the reading"; or, rather,
"that which ought to be read." The following names are
also given to it—*Al Kitab* (the Book), *Kitab Allah* (the
Book of God), *Kitab Atzig* (the precious Book), *Kalam
Cherif* (the Sacred Word), *Mahof* (the Supreme Code), *Al*

* The first edition of the 'Koran,' that of Alexander Paganini, of Brixan,
appears to have been published at Venice, about the year 1599, according to
some, but about 1515 or 1530, according to others. It was burnt by order

Furkan (that which distinguished what is good and true from what is evil and false), and *Tanzil* (descended from heaven).

The Koran is held by Mohammedans to be not only of divine origin, but also as eternal and uncreated; remaining, as some express it, in the very essence of God, on which account the Almighty made the miracle of Mohammed to consist in an inimitable style, as exhibited in the Koran. The first transcript of it has been from everlasting, near God's throne, written on a table of vast dimensions, called the *preserved Table* on which are also recorded the divine decrees—past, present, and to come. Mohammedans also believe that before all other things God created this *Table of His decrees*, and after that His *Kullum*, or pen: that this table is one entire precious stone of vast magnitude, and that the pen consists of one pearl, from whose slit is distilled the light that serves as the true and only ink employed by God, or rather by the angels, in obedience to His commands, in registering the words and deeds of men. A copy from this table, in one volume, on paper, was by the ministry of the angel Gabriel, sent down to the lowest heaven, in the month of Ramadan, on the night of power; from *whence* Gabriel revealed it to Mohammed, piecemeal, some portions at Mecca and some at Medina, at different times, during the space of twenty-three years, as the exigency of circumstances required; giving him, however, the consolation of seeing it, bound in silk and ornamented with the precious stones of Paradise, once in twelve months, a privilege which was doubled during the last year of his life.

---

of the Pope. Sale's translation into English, with its valuable introduction, is well known and duly appreciated. There are also French translations, one by Du Ruyter and the other by Savary. A translation by Ludovico Marraccius was not allowed to appear, unless accompanied by a *Prodomus ad refutationem Alcorani*, Padua, 1698. Not a single copy of Paganini's edition is now to be found in any library.

It is said that few chapters were delivered entire, the most part being revealed in detached portions, and written down, from time to time, by the Prophet's amanuensis, in such and such a chapter, until completed, according to Gabriel's directions. The first part that was revealed is generally agreed to have been the first five verses of the 96th chapter, as follows :—

" Recite thou, in the name of thy Lord who created—
  Created man from CLOTS OF BLOOD !
  Recite thou ! for the Lord is the most Beneficent,
    Who hath taught thee the use of the pen (to record Revelation),
    Hath taught man that which he knew not."

After the newly-revealed passages had been, from the Prophet's mouth, taken down in writing by his scribe, they were published to his followers, several of whom took copies for their private use, but the far greater number got them by heart. The originals, when returned, were put promiscuously into a chest, observing no order of time, for which reason it is uncertain when many passages were revealed.

The Koran is divided into 114 large portions of very unequal length, called by us chapters, or suras, but by the Arabians *sorah* in the singular, plural *sowar*.* These chapters are not in the manuscript copies distinguished by the numerical order, but by titles taken, sometimes, from a peculiar subject treated of, or a person mentioned therein, but usually from the first word of note. Some chapters have two or more titles occasioned by the difference of the copies, some of them having been said to have been revealed at Mecca, and others at Medina, the noting of which difference makes a part of the title. Each chapter is divided into smaller portions of very unequal length also,

* " It must be remarked that all the suras, or chapters, were intended not for *readers*, but for *hearers*—that they were all promulgated by public *recital*—and that much was left, as the imperfect sentences show, to the manner and suggestive action of the speaker."—The ' Koran,' translated by the Rev. J. M. Rodwell, M.A.

which are commonly called verses, the Arabic name being Ayát (sign or wonder). Next after this title, at the head of every chapter, excepting the ninth only, is prefixed the following solemn form, called by the Mohammedans "*Besmallah*"—"In the name of the Most High."*

The Koran has always been held by the Mohammedans as the greatest of all miracles, and equally stupendous with the act of raising the dead. The miracles of Moses and Jesus,† they say, were transient and temporary, but that of Mohammed is permanent and perpetual, and, therefore, far superior to all the miraculous events of preceding ages.

In a literary point of view, the Koran is the most poetical work of the East. The greater portion of it is in a rhymed prose, conformably to the taste which has, from the remotest times, prevailed in the above portion of the globe. It is universally allowed to be written with the utmost purity and elegance of language in the dialect of the tribe of the Koreish, the most noble and polite of all the Arabs, but with some mixture, although very rarely, of other dialects. It is, confessedly, the standard of the Arabian language, and abounds with splendid imagery and the boldest metaphors; and, notwithstanding that it is sometimes obscure and verging upon tumidity, is generally vigorous and sublime,

* The following is a metrical account of the verses, etc., of the Koran, aken from a very beautiful copy, once the property of the unfortunate Tippoo Sahib, but now preserved in the public library at Cambridge :—

> The verses of the Koran, which is good and heart delighting,
> Are six thousand, six hundred and sixty-six ;
> One thousand of it command, one thousand strongly prohibit,
> One thousand of it promise, one thousand of it threaten,
> One thousand of it read in choice stories ;
> And know, one thousand of it to consist in instructive parables,
> Five hundred of it in discussions, lawful and unlawful,
> One hundred of it in prayers for morn and even,
> Of such an one I have now told you the whole.

† Jesus Christ is revered by all the doctors as the greatest of the prophets before the Arabian legislator ; as the Messiah of nations and the Spirit of God. The Saviour is regarded as predestined to return in the plenitude of ages, to reassemble all men in unity of one belief." (D'Obson, vol. i. p. 305 See note †, p. 51.)

so as to justify the observation of the celebrated **Göthe, that** the Koran is a work with whose dulness the reader is at first disgusted, afterwards attracted by its charms, and finally, irresistibly ravished by its many beauties.

While Mohammed lived, the Koran was kept in loose sheets only. His successor, Abu-Bekr, first collected them into a single volume, not only from the palm leaves, skins, and shoulder-bones of mutton whereon they had been written, but also from the mouths of those who had committed them to memory; and, when the transcript was completed, the keeping of it was entrusted to Haphsa, the daughter of Omar, one of the widows of Mohammed, in order for its being consulted as an original. As, however, a considerable degree of diversity was found to exist between the several copies already dispersed throughout the provinces, Othman, the successor of Abu-Bekr, in the thirtieth year of the Hegira, procured a great number of them to be taken from that of Haphsa, suppressing, at the same time, all the others not conformable to the original.

In order properly to estimate the merits of the Koran, it should be considered that when the Prophet arose eloquence of expression and purity of diction were much cultivated, and that poetry and oratory were held in the highest estimation. "The miracle of the Koran," says a Mohammedan author, "consists in its elegance, purity of diction, and melody of its sentences, so that every Ajemer who hears it recited perceives at once its superiority over all other Arabic compositions. Every sentence of it inserted in a composition, however elegant, is like a brilliant ruby, and shines as a gem of the most dazzling lustre, while in its diction it is so inimitable as to have been the subject of astonishment to all learned men, ever since its first promulgation."

It was to the Koran so considered as a permanent miracle that Mohammed appealed as the chief confirmation of his mission, publicly challenging the most eloquent men in

Arabia, then abounding with persons whose sole study and ambition it was to excel in elegance of style and composition, to produce even one single chapter that might compete therewith.*

According to tradition, Lebid Abu Rabia, a native of Yehmen, and one of the seven whose verses constituted the Maallakat (a series of prizes suspended in the Kaaba), was still an idolator when Mohammed announced publicly his law. One of the poems began with the verse, "All praise is vain which referreth not unto God, and all good that proceedeth not from Him is but a shadow." For some time no poet could be found to compete with it, but at length the chapter of the Koran entitled *Barat* was affixed to a gate in the same temple, and Lebid was so overcome by the first few verses as to declare that they could only have been produced by the inspiration of God himself, and he forthwith embraced Islamism.†

The passage from the Koran which effected this conversion was the following :—

"There is nothing doubtful in this book : it is a direction to the pious who believe the mysteries of faith, who observe the appointed times of prayer, who distribute alms out of what We(God) have bestowed upon them ; who believe in the Revelation that hath been sent down unto thee (Mohammed), as well as in that delivered unto the Prophets before thee, and who have a firm assurance in the life to come ; such, verily, are under the guidance of their Lord, and they shall prosper."

* The statement that Mohammed composed the Koran by the aid of a Christian monk, and Abdallah Salam, a Persian Jew, refutes itself, for it is not to be credited that the excellence of the Arabian language should be derived from two foreigners of whom the one was a Syrian and the other a Persian.

† Lebid was afterwards of great service to Mohammed in answering the satires and invectives that were made upon and against him and his religion, by the infidels, and particularly by Amri, at Kais, prince of the tribe of Asad, and author of one of the seven poems called Al Maallakat.

" As for unbelievers . . . . they are like unto one who kindleth a fire, and when it hath thrown light upon every thing around him, shutteth his eyes. God taketh away their light, and leaveth them in darkness; they shall not see; they are deaf and dumb, and blind; therefore, will they not repent. Or, like unto a storm-cloud from heaven, fraught with darkness, thunder and lightning, they put their fingers in their ears, because of the noise of the thunder, for fear of death. God compasseth the infidels; the lightning doth all but blast them with blindness; so long as it enlighteneth them, they walk therein, but when the darkness cometh on, paralyzed they stand."*

The admiration with which the reading of the Koran inspires the Arabs is due to the magic of its style, and to the care with which Mohammed embellished his prose by the introduction of poetical ornaments; by his giving it a cadenced march and making the verses rhyme; its variety also is very striking, for sometimes, quitting ordinary language, he paints, in majestic verse, the Eternal, seated on His throne, dispensing laws to the universe; his verses become melodious and thrilling when he describes the everlasting delights of Paradise; they are vigorous and harrowing when he depicts the flames of hell.

The Koran is held by Mohammedans in the greatest reverence and respect. The more strict among them dare not touch it without being first washed or legally purified,† which, lest they should do, so, through inadvertence, they sometimes write these words on the book itself, or on its cover: " None shall touch it, but they who are purified." They read it reverentially, never holding it below their girdle; kiss it, upon first opening it; carry it with them in military expeditions; inscribe sentences from it upon their banners; adorn it with gold and precious stones;

* Chapter II.

† The Jews have a like veneration for their book, never presuming to touch it with unwashed hands.

and, knowingly, never suffer it to be in the possession of an unbeliever. It is made the foundation of their education, and the children in all schools are taught to chaunt it, and commit the whole of it to memory. It is admitted everywhere as the standard of all law and practice. Their judges swear by it.* All Mohammedans are bound to study it, in order to find therein the *light of their life*. They have mosques where the whole is read through, daily, thirty relays of *Korra* (readers) taking it up in succession. For twelve hundred years has the voice of this book been thus kept resounding, at all moments, through the ears and hearts of so many millions of men. There are instances of Mohammedan doctors who had read it through seventy thousand times.

The Koran repeatedly enjoins belief in one God, resignation to His will, and perfect obedience to His commands, charity, mildness, abstinence from spirituous liquors, and toleration, ascribing particular merit to dying in the cause of religion; while, as to practical duties, besides the obligation to propagate Islam, the first which are inculcated in the Koran, are prayers directed towards the temple of Mecca,† at five appointed hours of the day; fasting‡ during the month of Ramadan and' alms, to which the one-fortieth part of a person's property must be appropriated and bestowed even upon foes and the brute creation. Of these three chief duties Mohammed considered prayer so indispensable and necessary that he used to call it *the pillar of religion* and the *key to Paradise*; declaring also that there could be no good in any religion wherein there was no prayer. §

---

* This custom was introduced by the Emperors.

† This point is called the *Kebla*, and tables have been constructed for finding it when no other indication is to be had. (See page 31, note †.)

‡ According to the Mohammedan divines, there are three degrees of fasting :—1. The restraining the belly and other parts of the body from satisfying their lusts. 2. The restraining the ears, eyes, tongue, hands, feet, and other members from sin. And 3. The fasting of the heart from worldly cares, and refraining the thoughts from everything but God.

§ Of the comparative efficacy of these three duties it is said—Prayer

The injunction regarding washing and cleanliness is an accessory to prayer. Sale, in his ' Preliminary Dissertation,' p. 139, says : " That his followers might be more punctual in this duty, Mohammed is said to have declared that the practice of religion is founded on cleanliness, which is the one-half of the faith, and the key of prayer, without which it will not be heard by God. That these expressions may be the better understood, Al Ghazali reckons four degrees of purification ; of which the first is the cleansing of the body from all pollution, filth and excrement ; the second the cleansing of the members of the body from all wickedness and unjust actions ; the third, the cleansing of the heart from all blameable inclinations and odious vices ; and the fourth, the purging a man's secret thoughts from all affections which may divert their attendance from God ; adding, that the body is but the outward shell with respect to the heart, which is as the kernel. And for this reason he highly complains of those who are superstitiously solicitous in exterior purifications, avoiding those persons as unclean who are not so scrupulously nice as themselves, and at the same time have their minds lying waste and overrun with pride, ignorance and hypocrisy. Whence it plainly appears with how little foundation the Mahometans have been charged by some writers with teaching, or imagining that these formal washings alone cleanse them from their sins."

But the injunctions of the Koran were not confined to religious and moral duties. " From the Atlantic to the Ganges," says Gibbon, " the Koran is acknowledged as the fundamental code, not only of theology, but of civil and criminal jurisprudence, and the laws which regulate the actions and the property of mankind are governed by the immutable sanctions of the will of God." Or, in other words, the Koran is the general code of the Mohammedans ;

leads half-way to heaven ; Fasting carries the faithful to heaven's gate and Alms-giving gains them admittance.

a religious, social, civil, commercial, military, judicial, criminal, penal code; it regulates everything, from the ceremonies of religion to those of daily life; from the salvation of the soul to the health of the body; from the rights of all to those of each individual; from the interests of man to those of society; from morality to crime; from punishment here to that in the life to come.

The Koran, consequently, differs materially from the Bible, which, according to Combe, "contains no system of theology, but is composed chiefly of narratives, descriptions, sublime effusions of devotional emotions, and much sound morality, bound together by no striking logical connexion."* Nor is it, like the Gospels, to be considered merely as the standard by which the religious opinions, the worship, and the practice of its followers are regulated, but it is also a political system; for on this foundation the throne itself is erected, hence every law of the State is derived, and by this authority every question of life and property is finally decided.

Mohammed was so alive to the danger attending priest-hoods in political States, and of their tendency to corrupt all governments, that he disapproved of the allowance of any such institution, and desired that every Mussulman should possess a copy of the Koran, and *be his own priest;* a wise wish, in which the Prophet did but imitate the divinely inspired Jesus; for the only religion founded by the latter was a pure worship, a religion without priests and external observances, resting solely on the feelings of the heart, on the imitation of God. "Never," says M. Renan, "was there a man less a priest than Jesus; never was there a greater enemy than he to those forms which stifle religion under the pretext of protecting it." Again; " No hierarchy properly so called existed in the new sect. They were to call each other ' brother,' but Jesus absolutely proscribed

* ' Essay on the Relation between Science and Religion.'

titles of superiority, such as 'Rabbi,' 'master,' 'father': he (Jesus) alone being 'master,' and God alone being 'father.'

Islam, therefore, is without a priesthood. The doctors of the law are the doctors of divinity, because the law is the Koran: but they are not supported by tithes; their functions are not sacerdotal, but judicial. Their wealth is derived neither from Church property, nor from tithes, nor from State pensions. They are supported by judicial fees in litigated cases, amounting to 2½ per cent., and by the revenues of lands appropriated to the mosques. The doctors of the law, indeed, form a corporation no less authoritative than the Church in England, with this difference, *that there is no dissent.*

Mohammed's creed was likewise free from suspicion and ambiguity, and the Koran is a glorious testimony to the *unity* of God. Rejecting the worship of idols and men,* of stars and planets, on the rational principle that whatever is born must die; that whatever rises must set; and that whatever is corruptible must perish and decay, Mohammed's rational enthusiasm confessed and adored an infinite and eternal Being without form or place, without issue or similitude, present to our most secret thoughts, existing by the necessity of His own nature, and deriving from himself all intellectual perfection. These subjects thus announced, in the language of the Prophet (chapters 2, 57, 58), are firmly held and revered by his disciples, and defined with mathematical precision by the interpreters and expounders of the Koran. A philosophical theist might subscribe the popular creed of the Mohammedans.

The God of Nature has written His existence in all His works, and His law in the heart of man. To restore the knowledge of the one and the practice of the other has been

* The Mohammedans never say that God created man after his own image, holding it the highest impiety and presumption in any one to attempt to give any description of God's form.

the real or the pretended aim of the prophets of every age ; the liberality of Mohammed allowed to his predecessors the same credit which he claimed for himself, and the claim to inspiration was prolonged from the fall of Adam to the promulgation of the Koran. For the author of Christianity, the Mohammedans are taught by the Prophet to entertain a high and mysterious reverence (chapters 7, 10),* and the Latin Church has not disdained to borrow from the Koran the *immaculate conception* of Christ's virgin mother.† During 600 years was the way of truth, but the Christians insensibly forgot the example of their founder. The piety of Moses and of Christ rejoiced in the assurance of a future prophet more illustrious than themselves ; and the Evangelist's promise of the Paraclete or Holy Ghost, the Comforter, was prefigured in the name, and accomplished in the person, of the greatest and the last of God's prophets.

The first and principal article of the Koran is, as we have said, the *unity* of God, and the certainty of the mission of Mohammed, who gives himself the title of the prophet and messenger of God, as understood by Mohammed, the chief, or rather the only cause of his prophetic mission. "The Christians," said he, "having fallen into error, corrupted this dogma by introducing the doctrine of the Trinity ;‡

---

* As one among many other proofs of this, the following fact may be adduced. During the reign of Mahomet IV., the same whose Grand Vizier besieged Vienna in 1683, but was defeated by John Sobieski, King of Poland, a Christian priest had made profession of Islam, and, to prove his zeal, reviled our Saviour, applying to him the epithet of " impostor," which he had been accustomed to give to Mohammed. The Mussulmans, shocked at the outrage, carried him before the Divan, and he was ordered for immediate execution.

† See Sale's ' Koran,' chap. iii. p. 39, and note *d*. St. Ambrose and St. Augustine, two fathers of the Church, have employed the most obscene terms in their disputation respecting this mystery ; so much so, that a regard for decency will not permit us to quote them.

‡ The celebrated text of the three witnesses (John i. v. 7) which is the foundation of the doctrine of the Trinity, has been proved, by the labours of Newton, Gibbon, Porson, and others, to have been an interpolation ; and Calmet himself acknowledges *that this verse is not found in any* ancient

and God, who would not leave the essential truths without testimony, sent his prophet to re-establish them. This is the reason why, in the Koran, the Mohammedans give themselves the designation of " UNITARIANS," in opposition to the so-called " Orthodox Christians" who are denominated " ASSOCIANTS," because, according to Mohammed, they associate with God, other objects of adoration and religious worship. Thus (in chapter 3) Mohammed says, " O people of the Book,"—that is to say, " O Jews and Christians, let not your worship transgress just bounds; say naught that is contrary to truth, when you speak of God; Jesus, the Messiah, the son of Mary, is nothing more than a prophet of God.* Believe then in God and His prophets, and make no mention of the Trinity. Set just bounds to your discourses. *God is only one God; all praise be unto Him!* God hath no son."

Another great object of the Koran was to unite the professors of the three different religions then followed, in the knowledge and worship of one God, under the sanction of certain laws and ceremonies partly of ancient and partly of novel institutions enforced by the consideration of rewards and punishments both temporal and eternal, and to bring them all to the obedience of Mohammed as the prophet and ambassador of God, who, after repeated admonitions, promises and threats of former ages, was sent at last to establish and propagate God's religion upon earth, and to be acknowledged as Chief Pontiff in spiritual mat-

---

copy of the Bible. Jesus taught the belief in *One* God, but Paul, with the Apostle John, who was a Platonist, despoiled Christ's religion of all its unity and simplicity, by introducing the incomprehensible *Trinity* of Plato, or *Triad* of the East, and also by deifying two of God's attributes—namely, His Holy Spirit, or the *Agion Pneuma* of Plato ; and His Divine Intelligence, called by Plato the *Logos* (Word), and applied under this form to Jesus (John i.).

* " The Mussulmans are Christians, if Locke reasons justly, because they firmly believe the immaculate conception, divine character and miracles of the Messiah." (Sir William Jones, ' Asiatic Review,' vol. i. p. 275.)

ters, as well as supreme prince in temporal ones. The great doctrine, then, of the Koran is the "*unity*" of God, to restore which, Mohammed asserted, was the chief end of his mission, it being laid down by him that there never was nor ever can be more than one true, orthodox religion, that although the particular laws or ceremonies are only temporary and subject to alteration, according to the divine direction, yet the substance of it being eternal truth, is not liable to change, but continues immutably the same, and that whenever this religion became neglected or corrupted in essentials, God vouchsafed to re-inform and re-admonish mankind thereof by several prophets of whom Moses and Jesus were the most distinguished till the appearance of Mohammed.

Mohammed never gave himself out as the founder of a new religion, but, on the contrary, he maintains (chapters 2, 3, 16, 26, &c.) his religion to be that of Abraham, which was revealed to him (Mohammed) by the Angel Gabriel (chapter 33). The sole object of the Koran is that of correcting the Scriptures, which he accused the Jews and Christians of having falsified, especially in what concerned his mission (chapters 2, 3, 6, 10, 11, 12, 16, 37). According to tradition, the book (Koran) was brought to him by the Angel Gabriel, written upon the skin of the ram sacrificed by Abraham in the place of his son Isaac, and ornamented with gold, silk and precious stones, but, according to another version almost generally received among Christians, he composed it, with the aid of a Persian Jew named Rabbi Warada-Ebn-Nawal, and of a Christian monk, Abbot of the Nestorian convent of Adol Kaisi, at Bosra in Syria. This opinion is very ancient, since we see Mohammed opposing and indignantly repelling it (chapters 10, 11, 16, 25).*

The Koran teaches in the most explicit manner, the existence of one only God (chapters 2, 3, 4, 5, 6, 17, 18, 34, 37,

* See note. page 68.

39, 40, 42, 59); eternal, who was unbegotten and has no children; without equal (chapter 112), Creator of all things (chapters 16, 17), good and merciful (chapters 3, 5, 6, 10, 40), protecting those who are not ungrateful to Him (chapters 3, 9, 64), pardoning those who offend Him provided they repent (chapters 25, 110), Sovereign Judge at the day of resurrection (chapters 2, 14, 16, 17, 18, 22); He will render to every one, according to his works (chapters 2, 3, 4, 10, 28), that is, to the good, and to those who fight and die in his cause (chapter 22); eternal felicity, the voluptuous description of which may, for beauty, be compared with all that the imagination of poets has ever created (chapters 4, 7, 13, 15, 18, 32, 35), and especially (chapters 27, 38, 45, 52, 55, 56, 76, 88) to the wicked eternal punish-in a hell beyond conception horrible.*   With the dogma of the existence of a God are joined those of Providence (chapters 15, 16, 23, 29, 32) and predestination (chapters 13, 114).   The Koran also teaches the existence of angels (chapters 2, 7, 9), but it forbids that these as well as the Prophet should be objects of adoration (chapter 3).   Every man has two protecting angels, who watch over his actions (chapter 35).   Demons are the natural enemies of human kind (chapters 35, 36, 38).   The Mussulmans should also believe in the existence of good and bad genii, different degrees of angels and demons (chapters 26, 55), and above all, in the divine mission of Mohammed, but without regarding him as superior to other men in respect of his nature (chapters 17, 29).

The morality of the Koran has not been less unjustly attacked than its dogmas.   It condemns debauchery and excesses of every kind (chapters 4, 17), usury (chapter 2),

---

* The punishments of hell consisted in the damned being made to drink nothing but boiling and stinking water; to breathe nothing but exceedingly hot winds (things most terrible in Arabia); to dwell for ever in continual fire, intensely burning; and to be surrounded by and enveloped in a black, hot, salt smoke, as with a coverlet.

avarice and pride (chapters 4, 17, 18), slander and calumny
(chapter 104), covetousness (chapters 4, 33), hypocrisy
(chapters 4, 63), the thirsting after worldly goods (chapters
100, 102); it ordains, on the contrary, alms-giving (chapters 2, 3, 30, 50, 57, 90), filial piety (chapters 4, 17, 29, 46),
gratitude towards God (chapter 5), fidelity to engagements
(chapters 5, 16), sincerity (chapters 6, 17, 23, 83), justice
(chapters 5, 6), especially towards orphans (chapters 13, 90)
and without respect of persons (chapter 80), chastity and
decency even in words (chapters 24, 25), the ransoming of
captives (chapters 13, 90), patience (chapters 346, 374),
submission (chapter 3), benevolence (chapter 28), forgiveness of injuries (chapters 3, 16, 24, 43), the returning of
good for evil (chapter 23), and the walking in the path of
virtue, not with the view of obtaining the approbation of
the world, but for being acceptable unto God (chapter 22).

The Koran, as already said, is not only a religious code,
but contains, in addition, the civil laws of the Mohammedans, as the Pentateuch contains those of the Jews; it
restrains polygamy by limiting the number of wives to four
(chapter 4), prescribes the ceremonies to be observed at
marriages (chapters 2, 6), determines the matrimonial duties
of the married pair (chapter 4), even the length of the time
for suckling (chapter 2), that of widowhood (chapter 2), and
regulates the dowry and jointure (chapters 2, 4), as well
as the course to be pursued in separations and divorces
(chapters 2, 4, 65).   Inheritances, wills, guardianships, con-
tracts have not escaped the attention of the Prophet, who
treats of them in the same chapters as last mentioned.
Lastly, punishments are pronounced against false witnesses
(chapters 5, 9), prevarication in judges (chapter 5), fraud
(chapter 4), theft (chapter 5), homicide* (chapters 2, 4, 6, 25),
infanticide (chapters 6, 17), incest (chapter 4), immodesty
and adultery (chapters 4, 19, 24, 25).   Here Mohammed

---

* As a proof of the great humanity inculcated in the Koran, it may be

exhibits himself not only as an apostle but as a legislator, whence it may be fairly presumed that these laws were not promulgated until after the Hegira, or, at least, until his doctrine had already made great progress—perhaps even some of them were not given till after the conquest of Mecca.

Such is the Koran which has been received by Mohammedans with a degree of reverence rarely witnessed among Christians towards the Holy Scriptures. In it they view the whole code of religious belief, civil law and moral obligation. The belief which they generally profess as drawn from the Koran consists in the following leading points. Religion is divided into two branches, Imān (faith) and Din (practice). Faith includes belief in God, his angels, his revelations in the Koran, his prophets, the resurrection and day of judgment, and God's absolute decrees. Practice includes prayer, comprehending under this head the purifications necessary before prayer, alms-giving, fasting, and the pilgrimage to Mecca.*

In order fully to appreciate the difference between Christianity and Mohammedanism, it must be borne in mind that whereas the hold which the former has over its professors is naturally referred by them to its dogmas, thus causing religion and morals to be regarded as distinct from each other ; in the latter it is, on the contrary, not the dogmatic, but the practical portion which has influenced the moral, social, legal, and political ideas and circumstances of its believers. So that to the Mohammedan mind, patriotism,

mentioned that there can scarcely be found in it one capital punishment, except such as are denounced in wholesale warfare against unbelievers, as in the Mosaic code. The retaliation of blood for blood is softened into a money compensation ; civil offences merely affecting property are not heavily punished ; while towards the unfortunate debtor the law is strikingly lenient.

* The pilgrimage to Mecca was but a regulation, in accordance with previous habits, to maintain the unity of doctrine, and to refresh the zeal and ardour of its professors.

legality, tradition, constitution, right, are all included in
that one word—Islam !

Among many excellencies of which the Koran may justly
boast are two eminently conspicuous; the one being the
tone of awe and reverence which it always observes when
speaking of, or referring to, the Deity, to whom it never
attributes human frailties and passions; the other the total
absence throughout it of all impure, immoral and indecent
ideas, expressions, narratives, &c., blemishes, which, it is
much to be regretted, are of too frequent occurrence in
the Jewish Scriptures. So exempt, indeed, is the Koran
from these undeniable defects, that it needs not the slightest
castigation, and may be read, from beginning to end,
without causing a blush to suffuse the cheek of modesty
itself.

The religion thus established by the Koran is a stern
and severe monotheism : it has nothing abstract and indis-
tinct in its primary notion of the Godhead. Allah, so far
from being a mere philosophic first cause regulating the
universe by established laws, while itself stands aloof in
unapproachable majesty, is an ever-present, ever-working
energy. It is a religion, moreover, stripped of all controversy, and which, proposing no mystery to offer violence
to reason, restricts the imagination of men to the being
satisfied with a plain, invariable worship, notwithstanding
the fiery passions and blind zeal that so often transported
them beyond themselves. Lastly, it is a religion from
which all worship of saints and martyrs, relics and images,
all mystery and metaphysical subtlety, all monastic seclusion and enthusiastic penance is banished ; and which bears
internal proofs of having been the result of long and deep
meditation upon the nature of things, upon the state and
condition of the nations of the world at that time, and upon
the reconcilement of the objects of religion with those of
reason. No wonder, therefore, that such a worship should

supersede the idolatrous ceremonies of the Kaaba, the rites of Sabianism, and the altars of Zoroaster.

We now proceed to offer a few remarks upon Mohammedanism as based upon the Koran.

Islam has never interfered with the dogmas of any faith —never persecuted, never established an inquisition, never aimed at proselytism. It offered its religion, but never enforced it. "Let there be no violence in religion."* "Surely those who believe and those who Judaize, and Christians, and Sabians, whoever believeth in God, and the last day, and doeth that which is right, they shall have their reward with their Lord; there shall not come any fear upon them, neither shall they be grieved."† The acceptance of that religion, moreover, conferred equal rights with the conquering body and emancipated the vanquished states from the conditions which every conqueror, since the world existed up to the period of Mohammed, had invariably imposed. Islam put an end to infanticide then prevalent in the surrounding countries. It put an end to slavery, the adscription to the soil. It administered even-handed justice, not only to those who professed its religion, but to those who were conquered by its arms. It reduced taxation, the sole tribute to the state consisting of one-tenth. It freed commerce from charges and impediments, it freed professors of other faiths from all fixed contributions to their church or their clergy, and from all contributions whatsoever to the dominant creed. The repetition of a single phrase was the only form required or pledge exacted from proselytes; for circumcision was not, as is generally supposed, imperatively insisted upon.

A full explanation of the causes which contributed to the progress of Mohammedanism is not, perhaps, even in the present day, completely attainable; but it is possible to point out several of leading importance. In the first place, those

* ' Koran,' chapter ii. † Ibid.

just and elevated notions of the Divine nature and of moral
duties which pervade the Koran, and that were particularly
qualified to strike a serious and reflecting people, already,
perhaps, disinclined by intermixture with their Jewish and
Christian fellow citizens, to the superstitions of their ancient
idolatry; next the judicious incorporation of tenets, usages
and traditions from the various religions that existed in
Arabia : and, thirdly, the extensive application of the precepts of the Koran to all the legal transactions and all the
business of life. To these causes some authors have added
the indulgence to voluptuousness. But an unprejudiced
and candid mind will reject such a supposition, for it will
be found that Mohammed placed no reliance upon induce-
ments of this kind for the diffusion of his system. It is not
by the rules of Christian purity or European practice that
this point is to be judged. If polygamy was a prevailing
usage in Arabia, as it unquestionably was, its permission
gave no additional license to the proselytes of Mohammed
who will be found to have narrowed the unbounded liberty
of Oriental manners* in this respect, while his decided
condemnation of adultery and of incestuous connexions so
frequent among barbarous nations does not argue any
lax and accommodating morality. A devout Mussulman
exhibits much more of the stoical than the epicurean character ; nor can any one read the Koran without being
sensible that it breathes an austere and scrupulous spirit.
In fact, the founder of a new religion or sect is but little
likely to obtain permanent success by indulging the vices
and luxuries of mankind. The severity, therefore, of the
Mohammedan discipline may be reckoned as among the

---

* It must also be taken into consideration that a man, in order to avail
himself of Mohammed's permission to have four wives, must be rich in order
to maintain them according to his condition ; few, therefore, except great
lords and wealthy persons, avail themselves of the privilege, for which
reason a plurality of wives does not produce so much injury in Mohammedan
states, as we are generally in the habit of supposing.

other causes of success. Precepts of ritual observance being always definite and unequivocal, are less likely to be neglected after their observation has been acknowledged, than those of moral virtue. Thus, the long fastings, the pilgrimages, the regular prayers and ablutions, the constant almsgiving, the abstinence from stimulating liquors enjoined by the Koran, created a visible standard of practice among its followers and preserved a continual recollection of their law.

The fact that the Mohammedans connected their commerce with the advancement of the Koran may also be regarded as another cause, for the settlements they made in the East introduced it to the knowledge of princes who had, before, only a very imperfect idea of any religion. On parts of the Malabar coast, and at Malacca, the Mohammedans were favourably received. The kings of Ternate and Tidor, together with other Eastern princes, adopted their creed; and when the Moguls ruled over Candahar, Cambay, Gujerat and many other kingdoms, which had hitherto been jealous of the Mohammedan influence, they appear to have obtained some proselytes to the Koran.

When the Portuguese arrived in India they found the Mohammedan religion flourishing amid the superstitions of the Hindoos. It was recorded that the ancient Zamorin or emperor, whose principal residence was at Calicut, had, more than 600 years before their arrival, received the Moors with the greatest hospitality, and having introduced them into credit in his kingdom, had at last embraced their faith. *Sarama Payrimal,* the last of these princes, sailed in an Arabian vessel to end his days at Mecca.

Mohammed's intolerance has been designedly exaggerated. To idolators, indeed, or those who acknowledged no special revelation, one alternative only was proposed—conversion or the sword—*the people of the Book,* as they are termed in the Koran, or, the four sects of Christians, Jews,

G 2

Magians and Sabians, were permitted to redeem their adherence to their ancient law, by the payment of tribute and by other marks of humiliation and servitude.*   But the limits which Mohammedan intolerance had prescribed to itself were seldom transgressed, the word they pledged to unbelievers was rarely forfeited, and, with all their insolence and oppression, the Moslem conquerors were mild and tolerant in comparison with those who obeyed the Pontiffs of Rome and Constantinople.   So much so that it may be affirmed with certain truth, that if the Western princes had been lords of Asia instead of the Saracens and Turks, they would not have tolerated Mohammedanism as Mohammedans have tolerated Christianity, since they persecuted, with the most relentless cruelty, those of their own faith whom they deemed heterodox.† " It may be truly said," observes M. Jurieu, " that there is no comparison between the cruelty of the Saracens against the Christians and that of Popery against the true believers. In the wars against the Vaudois, or in the massacres alone on St. Bartholomew's day, there was more blood spilt on account of religion than was shed by the Saracens in all their persecutions of the Christians.   It is expedient to cure men of this prejudice, namely, that Mohammedanism is a cruel sect, which was propagated by putting men to their choice of death or the abjuration of Christianity. This is in no wise true; and the conduct of the Saracens was as evangelical meekness in comparison with

---

* " When tribute was once agreed to, whether voluntarily or by compulsion, the inhabitants were entitled to all their former privileges, including the free exercise of their religion.   When a sovereign consented to pay tribute, he retained his territory, and only became subject to the usual relations of a tributary prince."   (Elphinstone's ' History of India,' p. 261.)

† " Had the Saracens, Turks, and other Mohammedan tribes," says Chatfield ('Historical Review, p. 311), "adopted the same conduct towards the Christians as the European nations had practised towards the followers of the Koran, it is probable that the Christian religion would have been extinguished in the East.

that of popery, which exceeded the cruelty of the cannibals."

The religion of Mohammed, if not spiritual, was at least consistent and practical, and it was laid down, like a firm causeway across a quagmire of superstition and gnosticism, wherein the Christian name was profaned and the morality of nature put to the blush, so that there is no exaggeration in asserting that never in the course of their history have Mohammedans been brought into contact with any form of Christianity that was not too degenerate in its rites, its doctrines, and its effects to be worthy of their esteem.*

It is pretty clear that the mission of Moses was to the Israelites *alone,* and was, so far from being intended for any other nation, that the law respecting proselytes made it difficult for a stranger to be admitted into the congregation of the sons of Jacob, and it is also plain from the books attributed† to the Evangelists that the apostles had some doubts whether any but the Jews were to be admitted into the benefit of their new dispensation, though upon a consultation it was determined that the Gentiles should have the Gospel preached unto them. It is evident from Christian authors themselves that as soon as the Christian religion became established at court, it retained very little of that simplicity and purity which are visible in the Gospels. Pride, avarice, feuds, and factions divided the teachers of it, and never-ending wars were commenced by the pens of the writers of all sides. "Long before Constantine's time,"

* Smith and Dwight's ‘Missionary Researches,’ vol. ii. p. 334.

† "Each of the four Gospels," says M. Renan (‘Life of Jesus,’ Introduction, p. 8), "bears at its head the name of a personage known either in the Apostolic history, or in the Gospel history itself. These four personages are not strictly given to us as the authors. The formulas ‘according to St. Matthew,—according to St. Mark,—according to St. Luke,—according to St. John,’ do not imply that in the most ancient opinion these recitals were written from beginning to end by Matthew, Mark, Luke and John; they merely signify *that they were the tradition*, proceeding from each of these Apostles, and claiming their authority."

says Milton, "the generality of Christians had lost much of the primitive sanctity and integrity, both of their doctrine and manners. Afterwards, when he had enriched the church, they began to fall in love with honours and civil power, and the Christian religion went to wreck."

In the sixth century Mohammed appeared in the East and settled his religion, extirpating idolatry out of a great part of Asia, Africa, and Egypt, in all which parts the worship of the one true God remains to this day. The minds of the multitude were tempted by the invisible as well as temporal blessings of the Arabian prophet, and charity will hope that many of the proselytes entertained a serious conviction of the truth and sanctity of his revelation. In the eye of an inquisitive polytheist it must appear worthy of the human and the Divine nature. More pure than the system of Zoroaster, more liberal than the law of Moses, the religion of Mohammed might seem less inconsistent with reason than the creed of mystery and superstition which in the seventh century disgraced the simplicity of the Gospel.

The most convincing proof of the power of Mohammed's religion over the minds of its professors may be found in the fact that although Islam is old enough to have experienced that decrepitude of all other beliefs—the putting the *creature* in the place of the *Creator*—its followers have firmly withstood the temptation of reducing the object of their faith and devotion to a level with the senses and the imagination of men, and have remained free from bigotry and superstition, never disgracing the intellectual image of the Deity by any visible idol. "I believe in one God, and in Mohammed the apostle of God," is the simple and invariable profession of Islamism.

It is a monstrous error to suppose, as some have done, and others still do, that the faith taught by the Koran was propagated by the sword alone, for it will be readily admitted by all unprejudiced minds, that Mohammed's religion,—by which prayers and alms were substituted for the blood of human victims, and which, instead of hostility and perpetual feuds, breathed a spirit of benevolence and of the social virtues, and must, therefore, have had an important influence upon civilisation,—was a real blessing to the Eastern world, and, consequently, could not have needed exclusively the sanguinary means so unsparingly and so unscrupulously used by Moses for the extirpation of idolatry.

How idle and ridiculous was it, therefore, to bestow nothing but insolent opprobrium and ignorant declamation upon one of the most powerful instruments which the hand of Providence has raised up to influence the opinions and doctrines of mankind through a long succession of ages. The whole subject, whether viewed with relation to the extraordinary rise and progress, either of the founder personally or of the system itself, cannot be otherwise than one of the deepest interest, nor can there be any doubt, but that of those who have investigated and considered the comparative merits of Mohammedanism and Christianity, there are few who have not at times felt confounded at the survey, and been compelled not only to admit that even the former must have been ordained for many wise and beneficent purposes, but even to confide in its instrumentality in the production, at least, of much eventual good.

CHAPTER II.

THE correctness of the observation with which we concluded the foregoing chapter will be rendered more evident from the following facts and considerations.

No nation, perhaps, ever existed which felt and expressed, early and late, a deeper reverence for the cause of learning than the Arabians. "No sooner," says a Mohammedan poet "do I see a learned man than I long to prostrate myself before him, and kiss the dust of his feet." Both the written and the traditional law came in aid to this praiseworthy sentiment:—"Equally valuable are the ink of the doctor and the blood of the martyr;" "Paradise is open to him who leaves behind him his pens and his ink," in other words, who commends learning by his example to his descendants; "The world is supported by four things only, the learning of the wise and the justice of the great, the prayers of the good and the valour of the brave." But what is still stronger, they introduce the Supreme Being Himself, in the Koran, calling riches a trivial, but learning an invaluable, good. Mohammed himself recommended it with singular earnestness, and his son-in-law, Ali, acknowledged the justice of the providential dispensation which withheld riches and imparted knowledge. The first revivers of philosophy and the sciences, the link, as they have been termed, between ancient and modern literature, were, most undoubtedly, according to every species of testimony, the Saracens of Asia and the Moors of Spain under the Abasside and Ommiade Caliphs. Letters which originally came to Europe from the East were brought thither, a second time, by the genius of Mohammedanism. It is well known that arts and sciences flourished among the Arabians for almost six hundred years; whilst among us, rude barbarism reigned and literature became almost extinct.

" According to the unanimous accounts," says Mosheim, " of the most credible witnesses, nothing could be more melancholy and deplorable than the darkness that reigned in the western world during this (the tenth) century, which, with respect to learning and philosophy, at least, may be called the *iron* age of the Latins. . . . . . The philosophy of the Latins extended no further than the single science of logic or dialectics, which they looked upon as the sum and substance of all human wisdom. It is certain that the Arabian philosophers had already founded numerous schools in Spain and Italy, whither numbers of enquirers after knowledge repaired and having adopted the Arabian philosophical tenets and systems, introduced them into the Christian schools." And, again, " It must be owned, that all the knowledge, whether of physic, astronomy, philosophy or mathematics which flourished in Europe from the tenth century was originally derived from the Arabian schools; and that the Spanish Saracens, in a more particular manner

may be looked upon as the fathers of European philosophy."
To the Arabs, modern Europe is indebted for its first bud
of poetic imagination and of its visions of romance. Turning
to good account the advantages obtained from their conquest of other nations, it was not long before they formed a
language and a literature of their own ; and having so done,
the rapidity of their intellectual progress, when compared
with that of the peoples preceeding them was wonderful.
It was eight centuries before the literature of Greece was
formed ; as many were necessary for the Roman world to
produce its great writers and poets. The same period
elapsed from the formation of the Roman provençal of the
South of France, until that nation could boast a literature
of its own. It was barely more than one hundred and fifty
years from the Hegira that the Arabs had become a people
advanced in letters and the conservators of ancient philosophy, poetry and art.

It had occupied the Roman and the Goth each a period,
including the greater part of two hundred years, to complete the subjugation of Spain. In twenty years the Arabs
had subdued the peninsula and advanced across the Pyre-
nees into the heart of France. Their influence in learning
was no less rapid and remarkable than their arms.

Ali, the nephew of the Prophet, and the fourth of the
Caliphs, first extended his patronage and protection to
letters. Under Moawyah, in whom the Caliphate became
hereditary, the Arabs collected the sciences of the Greeks.
After him, Abu Giafar Almansor, the second caliph of the
Abasside dynasty, seems to take the lead in the patronage
of learning and the sciences. Amidst several insurrections
and many splendid conquests, he still found time, taste and
money for a liberal encouragement of the arts, and founded
a metropolis, Bagdad, unequalled for magnificence and
population, and which continued to be the seat of his
descendants for above five hundred years. His grandson,

Haroun al Raschid, so dreaded by the Greeks for his valour and military skill, was better known in Europe and more deservedly celebrated there for the arts of peace, his love of science, and his encouragement of learning. He was the friend and correspondent of Charlemagne, the studious enquirer, the liberal patron, the importer of useful mechanical inventions into the barbarous nations that lay beyond him. But to Almammon, his son, must be awarded the palm of having laid the foundation of the literary fame of the Arabians. Hundreds of camels laden with MSS. were to be seen continually arriving at his court. From Seville to Ispahan their literary treasures were quickly spread. Bagdad and Cufa, with Bassora, Cairo, Fez and Morocco, Cordova, Granada and Valencia, with Seville, ere long, heard the eloquence of the academy and the pulpit. Philosophy spread more rapidly to the West, especially that of Aristotle, whom the Arabs almost worshipped as a God. The sciences were cultivated, the literature of Greece and Rome lived again in Arabian MSS. Poetry, confined, however, to the lyric and didactic, with love-songs innumerable abounded, as well as rhyme, either immediate or alternate. Such were the brilliant lights which were shed from the Arabian schools from the ninth to the fourteenth centuries.

The next most distinguished Mohammedan patrons of learning were the Abdalrhamans of Spain, descendants of Abdalrhaman, who established the Ommiade dynasty in that country in A.D. 749. Of these princes there appears to have been three, of whom the greatest was the third and last of that name. He was the eighth Caliph, and was the first who assumed the title of Emir Almoumenin (Commander of the Faithful). In his reign those political divisions which soon proved fatal to the dynasty had risen to an alarming height, and afforded sufficient trial to his wisdom and courage ; but he found time and opportunity to practise, on all occasions, a zealous attachment to learning. The long reign of more than fifty years, happening, too, in the tenth century, when Europe lay plunged in the grossest ignorance, while it necessarily advanced the literature of his own country, diffused some gleams of light on our intellectual darkness. The schools of Bagdad, Bocchara, and Bassora, however celebrated, were too distant to tempt the curiosity of European travellers and students; and had not Spain, under this generous protector, opened its academies and seminaries, the benefits of Arabian learning might have been faintly felt, or irreparably lost. Of the arts Abdalrhaman was a splendid cultivator, and in the magnificence of his courts, the architecture of his palaces, and the disposition of his gardens, he equalled, if not excelled, his Eastern competitors. The Zehra, a city and palace, three miles from Cordova, was the labour of twenty-five years, at the cost of six millions sterling. His seraglio comprised an establishment of above six thousand persons, and his hunting attendants were a formidable army of twelve thousand cavaliers.

A short digression is here necessary for the purpose of refuting the charge brought against the Caliph Omar, of having, in the year A.D. 641 ordered his lieutenant Amrou to destroy the Alexandrian library, by making its valuable MSS. serve as fuel for heating the public baths of that city; a charge the more preposterous, as it is well known that the *library of the Ptolemies*, with its four or seven hundred thousand volumes, was burned during a military operation of Julius Cæsar. That this accusation, so confidently repeated by one historian after another, is wholly unfounded, is moreover proved—firstly, by the fact that such a deed would have been a violation of the law of Mohammed, which expressly enjoins that the religious books of the Jews and Christians acquired by the right of conquest, should never be destroyed, and that the productions of profane science, history, poetry, philosophy, etc., may be lawfully made use of for the benefit of the faithful; secondly, that Albufaraj,* from whose "dynasties" the relation of the burning is taken, lived 600 years after the alleged event, whilst annalists of a much earlier date, Christians and natives of Egypt, have been perfectly silent on the subject; thirdly, that Saint Croix, who published his learned researches upon the libraries of Alexandria, pronounces it to be a mere fable, for the oldest and most considerable libraries at Alexandria did not exist further back than the fourth century.

That modern authors are to be found still repeating this myth, is the more surprising since the historian Gibbon has thrown doubt upon the story, on account of its own improbability and its absence of contemporary authority for it, either Christian or Mussulman; and has said that, even " if the ponderous mass of Arabian and Monophysite controversy were indeed consumed in the public baths, a philosopher may allow, with a smile, that it was ultimately devoted to the benefit of mankind."

But supposing it to be true that the Saracens did burn the Alexandrian library, how can this be made a charge by those who evinced no indignation at the burning, by Cardinal Ximenes, of all the Arab works on history, medicine and agriculture, on the ground that they were Alcorans; or at a like destruction of the Summer Palace, and the still far greater loss, by that vandalic act, of ancient monuments and uninterrupted records of the Chinese Empire, &c. &c. ?

But to resume : Europe is still further indebted to Mohammedanism, for, not to mention that to the struggles during the Crusades we mainly owe the abolition of the onerous parts of the feudal system, and the destruction of those

* The tale of Abulfaraj would not have been so industriously circulated, had it not served the purpose of those who wished to impute to the barbarians of Rome the guilt of darkening the world. (See Gibbon, vol. vi., p. 66, note by Editor. Bohn's edition.)

aristocratic despotisms on the ruins of which arose the proudest bulwark of our liberties, Europe is to be reminded that she is indebted to the followers of Mohammed, as the link which connects ancient and modern literature; for the preservation, during a long reign of Western darkness, of the works of many of the Greek philosophers; and for the cultivation of some of the most important branches of science, mathematics, medicine, etc., which are highly indebted to their labours. Spain, Cassino, and Salernum were the nurseries of the literature of the age; and the works of Avicenna, Averroes, Beithar, Abzazel and others, gave new vigour and direction to the studies of those who were emerging from a state of barbarism. Their zeal in the pursuit of geographical knowledge impelled them to explore and found kingdoms even in the desert regions of Africa. Through its brightest periods, nay, even from its origin, Mohammedanism was, comparatively, favourable to literature. Mohammed himself said "that a mind without erudition was like a body without a soul; that glory consists not in wealth, but in knowledge;" and he charged his followers to seek for learning in the remotest parts of the globe.

The Caliphate was held, for several ages, by a race of monarchs who rank among the most accomplished by whom any sceptre has been swayed. Religious differences were forgotten: "I chose this learned man," said the Caliph Almammon, speaking of Mussul, a Christian whom he was blamed for making president of a college at Damascus, "not to be my guide in religious matters, but to be my teacher of science."

Who has not mourned over the fate of the last remnant of chivalry, the fall of the Mussulman empire in Spain? Who has not felt his bosom swell with admiration towards that brave and generous nation of whose reign for eight centuries, it is observed even by the historians of their enemies, that not a single instance of cold-blooded cruelty is recorded? Who has not blushed to see a Christian priesthood goading on the civil power to treat with unexampled bigotry and devilish cruelty, a people from whom they had always received humanity and protection; and to record the political fanaticism of Ximenes in consigning to the flames the labours of the philosophers, mathematicians, and poets of Cordova, the literature of a splendid dynasty of seven hundred years.

It is in the compositions of Friar Bacon, who was born in 1214, and who learned the Oriental languages, that we discover the most extensive acquaintance with the Arabian authors. He quotes Albumazar, Thabet-Ebu-Corah, Ali Alhacer, Alkandi, Alfraganus and Arzakeb; and seems to have been as familiar with them as with the Greek and Latin classics, especially with Avicenna, whom he calls " the chief and prince of philosophy."* The great Lord Bacon, it is well known, imbibed and borrowed the first principles of his famous experimental philosophy from his predecessor and namesake Roger Bacon, a fact which indisputably establishes the derivation of the Baconian philosophical system from the descendants of Ishmael and disciples of Mohammed.

In reply to the almost stereotyped assertion that " Mohammedanism is in the present day an enemy to science and letters, it has been observed, that so far from this being the truth, Islam has outstripped the enlightenment of our age by making instruction a fundamental law. Every child must be put to school in its fifth year. It is the duty of the State to instruct the citizen, that he may understand the laws he has to obey, and of the family to teach the child the means by which he may acquire his livelihood. Every scholar is instructed in a handicraft, and some of them have earned thereby their subsistence. There have been, however, no educational heart-burnings, because each commonalty had to teach its children for and by itself. At Constantinople,

* See Sharon Turner's ' History of England during the Middle Ages,' vol. iv., p. 418.

when a quarter is burned down, which is by no means an unfrequent occurrence, the inhabitants are obliged to rebuild the school, but the mosque is not restored until provided by its own endowments, or by some pious persons."*

Another assertion, viz. that modern Turkey is a despotic country, will, if examined, be found as void of truth as the one above, for " Turkey is the only government in the world which is not struggling with its people to wrench from them their privileges. It is, on the contrary, engaged in an attempt to confer them. A Sultan can impose no tax, make no law, declare no war, contract no debt. If the constitution of Islam were translated and applied to any country in Europe, it would be considered a beautiful but impracticable theory of Utopian freedom."†

As for the military exploits of the Mussulmans, they are, without doubt, the most glorious recorded in history. What can be found more wonderful than the empire of the Saracens, which extended from the Straits of Gibraltar as far as India ? See the Turks on one side and the Tartars on the other, who preserve the grandeur and the renown of Mohammed ! Find, if it be possible, among the conquering Christian princes, any that can be put in the balance with the Saladins, the Gengis Khans, the Tamerlanes, the Amuraths, the Bajazets, the Mahomets II., and the Solymans. Did not the Saracens confine Christianity within the bounds of the Pyrennean mountains ? Did they not assail Italy, and proceed as far as the heart of France ? Did not the Turks extend their conquests to the confines of Germany and the Gulf of Venice ? The leagues, the crusades of Christian powers, those grand expeditions which drained the Latin church of men and money, can they not be compared to a sea whose waves flow from the west to the east, to be broken when they encounter the Mohammedan power as against some towering and stupendous rock ?

* See ' The East and the West,' p. 178.
† Ibid., p. 184.

Still more wonderful were the naval triumphs of this extraordinary people; in the days of Mohammed so dreaded was the sea by the Arabs, that he declared its intervention would be a valid excuse for not performing the pilgrimage to Mecca. A generation had not passed away when their flag floated triumphantly in the Mediterranean. Crete was taken, and the islands in the south of the Archipelago shared its fate; Sicily fell a prey to the Mohammedans of northern Africa, who also obtained permanent settlements in Corsica, Sardinia and the south of Italy.

The Saracens for a long time maintained a naval superiority in the Mediterranean, whether for the purposes of war or of commerce, some of their vessels being of a very large size. About the year 970 Abdalrahman, the Saracen Sultan or Caliph of the greater part of Spain, built a vessel larger than any that had ever been seen in those parts, and loaded her with innumerable articles of merchandise to be sold in the Eastern regions. Meeting on her way with a ship carrying despatches from the Emir of Sicily to Almoez, a sovereign on the African coast, she seized and pillaged it. On this Almoez, who was also sovereign of Sicily, which he governed by an emir or viceroy, fitted out a fleet, that took the great Spanish ship as it was returning from Alexandria, laden with rich wares for Abdalrahman's own use. Many other instances of ships of a very large size having been constructed by the Saracens have been recorded; and it has been suggested as highly probable, that it was in imitation of those ships that the Christian Spaniards introduced the use of large ones, for which they were distinguished during the reign of Philip II., whose "invincible Armada" consisted of ships much larger than the English vessels opposed to them.

No treatment can be more unjust than that which Mohammedanism has received at the hands of English writers of Indian history. Thus, they contrast the Mogul Emperors

H

of the fourteenth century with "the victorious, mild and merciful progress of the British arms in the East in the nineteenth." But if their object were a fair one, they should contrast the Mussulman invasion of Hindostan with the contemporaneous Norman invasion of England—the characters of the Mussulman Sovereigns with those of their contemporaries in the West—their Indian wars of the fourteenth century with our French wars or with the Crusades—the effect of the Mohammedan conquest upon the character of the Hindoo, with the effect of the Norman Conquest upon the Anglo-Saxon, "when to be called an Englishman was considered as a reproach—when those who were appointed to administer justice were the fountains of all iniquity—when magistrates whose duty it was to pronounce righteous judgments were the most cruel robbers—when the great men were inflamed with such a greed for money that they cared not by what violence they acquired it—when the licentiousness was so great that a princess of Scotland found it necessary to wear a religious habit in order to preserve her person from violence."*

The history of the Mohammedan dynasties in India is full, it is said, of lamentable instances of the cruelty and rapacity of the early conquerors, not without precedent, however, in contemporary Christianity, for when Jerusalem was taken by the first Crusaders† under Godfrey de Bouillon at the close of the tenth century, the garrison, consisting of 40,000 men, was put to the sword, without distinction; arms protected not the brave, nor submission the timid; no

---

* Henry of Huntingdon and Eadmer.

† Speaking of the Crusades, Clarke observes :—"Morals certainly reaped no benefit from them ; for of all the armies of any age or nation, none seem ever to have surpassed in profligacy and licentiousness those of the Holy Wars. The Crusades fixed a stamp of permanency on popular superstition ; they encouraged the utmost violence of fanaticism ; war became a sacred duty ; and, instead of prayer and acts of benevolence, the slaughter of human beings was inculcated as an expiation for offences." ('Vestigia Anglicana,' vol. i. p. 339.)

age or sex received mercy; infants perished by the same sword that pierced their mothers. The streets of Jerusalem were covered with heaps of slain, and the shrieks of agony and despair resounded from every dwelling. When Saladin, the Soldan of Egypt and Syria, retook it in the second crusade, *no lives were lost after the surrender,* and he showed the greatest kindness to the Christian captives, *giving those who were poor their liberty without ransom.* Before the name and morals of this illustrious man the pretensions of Philip of France, and even the renown of Richard himself, fade away. Possessing some literature and more science, he ever, during the progress of his conquests, respected the arts. Whilst he practised towards himself the restraint and abstinence of an ascetic, towards others his indulgence and liberality were unbounded. Clemency and other virtues were exemplified in his person, and his life exhibited a character which his rivals would have done well to imitate, and which would not have disgraced any aspirant to Christian excellence. " The Soldan was doubtless a person of eminent bravery, wisdom and generosity; he died, soon after the truce, at Damascus, bequeathing alms to be distributed among the poor, *without distinction of Jew, Christian or Mussulman.*"* Now, mark the contrast. The Christian hero, Richard I., was a Sovereign whose splendour and magnificence were maintained by immense sums extorted from his subjects by the most unjustifiable means. His avarice was insatiable, and an unbridled lust impelled him not only to neglect his beautiful Queen Berengaria, daughter of Sancho, King of Navarre, but even to a nameless sin. A poor hermit upbraided him with his detestable crime before the whole Court, conjuring him, in God's name, to reflect on the destruction of Sodom.†

Most of the Sovereigns of the Mussulman dynasties were

---

* 'Vestigia Anglicana,' vol. i. p. 337.
† Rapin, p. 400.

men of extraordinary character. The prudence, activity and enterprise of Mahmoud of Ghizni, and his encouragement of literature and the arts were conspicuous. He showed so much munificence to individuals of eminence that his capital exhibited a greater assemblage of men of genius than any other monarch in Asia has ever been able to collect together. If rapacious in acquiring wealth, he was unrivalled in the judgment and grandeur with which he knew how to expend it. His four immediate successors were patrons of literature, and acceptable to their subjects as good governors. Can as much be said for their contemporaries, William the Norman and his descendants?

When Louis VII. of France, in the twelfth century, made himself master of the town of Vitri, he ordered it to be set on fire; in consequence of which inhuman command, 1,300 persons perished in the flames. In England, at the same time, under King Stephen, civil war was carried on with so much fury that the land was left uncultivated, and the implements of husbandry were destroyed or abandoned; while the result of our French wars in the fourteenth century was a state of things more horrible and destructive than had ever been experienced in any age or country. The insatiable cruelty of the Mohammedan conquerors, it is said, stands recorded upon more undeniable authority than the insatiable benevolence of the Mohammedan conquerors. We have abundant testimony of the cruelty of contemporary Christian conquerors; have we *any* evidence of their benevolence?

Feroze Shah III. ascended the throne in 1351, and distinguished himself by many useful public works, consisting of fifty dams across rivers, to promote irrigation, forty mosques and thirty colleges, one hundred caravansaries, thirty reservoirs, one hundred hospitals, one hundred public baths, one hundred and fifty bridges, besides many other edifices for pleasure and ornament, and, above all, the canal from the point in the Jumna, where it leaves the mountains in Carnoul, to Hansi and Hissa.

Baber, the first Sovereign of the Mogul dynasty, was the most engaging of men, and one of the noblest that ever lived or that ever entered India, and appears with as much simplicity as dignity. The stains of vices which disgraced his youth were wiped away, in the eyes of men, by the moral fortitude that enabled him to overcome them, and to become distinguished by the purity of his after life. He was an obedient son, a kind father and brother, a generous friend and placable enemy ; he was majestical yet affable, temperate in his diet, sparing in sleep, skilful in making gems, casting ordnance, and in other mechanical arts. He was bold, frank, open-handed and high-minded, scorning the national love of intrigue. His tastes were refined, his mind cultivated, his knowledge extensive, and, considering the circumstances of his birth and training, it redounds to his immortal honour that his life was,

> " Like rivers that water the woodlands,
> Darken'd by shadows of earth, but reflecting an image of heaven,"

Humayon, his son, whose character was free from violent passions and unstained by vices, was defeated and driven from Hindoostan by Shir Shah, an Afghan Prince, who took possession of the throne, and, after reigning five years, left the crown to his son Adil Shah ; nor was it till after a period of sixteen years that Humayon succeeded in recovering his rights. Shir Shah, the successful usurper, was a Prince of consummate prudence and ability, and notwithstanding his constant activity in the field during a short reign, had brought his territories into the highest order, and introduced many improvements into his civil government. He made a high road, extending for four months' journey, from Bengal to the Western Rhotas near the Indus, with caravansaries at every stage, and wells at every mile and a half. There was an imam and a muezzin at every mosque, with attendants of proper castes for Hindoos as well as for Mohammedans. The road was planted with rows of trees for shade, and in many places was in the state described, when seen by travellers, after it had stood eighty-two years.

It is almost superfluous to dwell upon the character of the celebrated Akber, who was alike great in the cabinet and the field, and renowned for his learning, toleration, liberality, courage, clemency, temperance, industry and magnanimity; but it is to his internal policy that Akber owes his place in that highest order of princes whose reigns have been a blessing to mankind. He forbade trials by ordeal and marriages before the age of puberty, and the slaughter of animals for sacrifice. He also permitted widows to marry a second time, contrary to Hindoo law. Above all, he positively prohibited the burnings of Hindoo widows against their will. He employed his Hindoo subjects equally with Mohammedans, abolished the capitation tax on infidels as well as all taxes on pilgrims, and strictly prohibited the making slaves of persons taken in war. He perfected all the financial reforms which had been commenced by Shir Shah. He caused all the lands capable of cultivation within the empire to be re-measured, ascertained the produce of each begah (somewhat more than half an acre), determined the proportion to be paid by the public, commuting the same for a fixed money rent, giving the cultivator the option of paying in kind if he thought the money rate too high. He abolished, at the same time, a vast number of vexatious taxes and office fees.

The result of these wise measures was to reduce the amount of the public demand considerably. His directions to his revenue officers have come down to us, and show his anxiety for the liberal administration of his system and for the ease and comfort of his subjects. The tone of his instructions to his judicial officers was just and benevolent.

He enjoined them to be sparing in capital punishments, and, unless in cases of dangerous sedition, to inflict none until the Emperor's confirmation had been received. He forbade mutilation or other cruelty as the accompaniment of capital punishments. He re-formed and new modelled his army, paying his troops in cash from the treasury instead of by assignments on the revenue. Besides fortifications and other public works, he erected many magnificent buildings which have been described and eulogized by the late Bishop Heber.* System and method were introduced into every part of the public service, and the whole of his establishments present an astonishing picture of magnifi cence and good order, where unwieldy numbers are managed without disturbance, and economy is attended to in the midst of profusion.

The distinguished Italian traveller, Pietro del Valle, also, who visited India during the reign of Jehanghir, Akber's son, and who wrote a description of his visit, in 1623, bears testimony to the character of that prince, as well as to the condition of the people under his rule, whom he found living, not only in a comfortable and even splendid manner, but also in perfect security; becanse the King, knowing that his subjects were inclined to such vanities, did not persecute them with false accusations, but took delight in seeing them living in splendour, and with every appearance of wealth.

But the reign of Shah Jehan, the grandson of Akber, was the most prosperous ever known in India. His own dominions enjoyed almost uninterrupted tranquillity, and good government, and although Sir Thomas Rowe was struck with astonishment at the profusion of wealth displayed when he visited the Emperor in his camp in 1615, in which at least two acres of ground were covered with silk, gold carpets and hangings, as rich as velvet embossed with gold

* Travels, vol. ii. p. 81-7.

and precious stones could make them, yet we have the testimony of Tavernier that he who caused the celebrated peacock throne to be constructed, who, at the festival of his accession, scattered among the bystanders money and precious things equal to his own weight, " reigned not so much as a king over his subjects, but more as a father over his family." His vigilance over his internal government was unremitting, and for the order and arrangement of his territory, and the good administration of every department of the State, no prince that ever reigned in India could be compared to Shah Jehan.

It was during the reign of this magnificent prince that the famous Delhi canal was constructed under the superintendence of his architect, Ali Murdan Khan. After having ministered to the necessities of the husbandmen, during a course of several hundred miles, this magnificent aqueduct was made subservient to the luxury and taste of the imperial city. A thousand streams flowed from its solid bed on either side, and spreading themselves through masonry channels, into every quarter of Delhi, disported, in varied shapes, through marble jets, or cooled the fevered limbs in sculptured baths, or trickled over the gorgeous flowers in harems, lawns and terraces ; or, anon, flowed to the humble houses of labourers, and slaked the poor man's thirst, and bathed the poor man's brow.

Thus, although it has been asserted, but not proved, that the Mohammedan rulers of India wrung as much from the inhabitants as has been taken by their English successors, the advocates of the former may, at least maintain, what cannot be advanced by the latter, that they gave full value for what they took ; that they administered a full measure of justice, high and low ; that the trader could convey his goods many hundreds of miles along roads at all times safe and in good repair ; and that whatever fault may be found with this system, the bulk of the people lived, in those times, in comparative affluence and security. That this must have been so, the moss-grown marble terraces, the stagnant water-courses, the owl-inhabited mansions and temples, the solitary pillar and arch, sufficiently attest. In fact, it may be asserted without fear of contradiction, that each of those so-called *barbarous* sovereigns expended as much money in works of public utility as would have supported any of the standing armies in these days.

It may not be altogether uninstructive to compare the noble and enduring works of these Eastern princes with the progress made in a like direction in our own country, or, indeed, in any western kingdom, at that period. The two pictures, it is greatly to be feared, would not bear comparison. In this country, we know, at any rate, that at the epoch alluded to, we possessed not a single canal; that our roads were, with few exceptions, mere cattle-tracks; that our largest cities could not boast of the supply of water, or of the police protection accorded to the humblest towns within the empire of Delhi; nor had an English traveller, journeying from London to Highgate, in those early days, so great a certainty of reaching his destination in safety, as had any of Shah Jehan's meanest subjects in travelling from the Punjaub frontier to Delhi, or from the latter city to Allahabad.

Mr. Holwell gives us an account of the people of Bengal under their native sovereigns, which might be deemed even fabulous, did it not come from one who had been long resident in the country, and who spoke from an intimate acquaintance with the subject.

" In truth," says that gentleman, " it would be almost cruelty to molest this happy people, for in this district are the only vestiges of the beauty, purity, piety, regularity, equity and strictness of the ancient Hindostan government. Here the property, as well as the liberty of the people, are inviolate. Here, no robberies are heard of, either public or private. The traveller, either with or without merchandise, becomes the immediate care of the government, which allots him guards, without any expenses, to conduct him from stage to stage; and these are accountable for the safety and accommodation of his person and effects. At the end of the first stage he is delivered over, with certain benevolent formalities, to the guards of the next, wno, after interrogating the traveller as to the usage he had received in his journey, dismiss the first guard with a written certificate of their behaviour, and a receipt for the traveller and his effects, which certificate and receipt are returnable to the commanding officer of the first stage who registers the same and regularly reports it to the Rajah.

" In this form, the traveller is passed along through the country, and if he only passes, he is not suffered to be at any expense for food, accommodation or carriage for his merchandise or luggage; but it is otherwise if he is permitted to make any residence in one place above three days, unless occasioned by sickness or any unavoidable accident. If anything is lost in this district,—for instance, a bag of money or other valuable,—the person who finds it hangs it on the next tree, and gives notice to the nearest choutry or place of guard, the officer of which orders immediate publication of the same by beat of tom-tom, or drum."*

It will now be shown, by way of contrast, what was the state of *Christian* and *enlightened* England, during the reigns of the sovereigns contemporaneous with the above-named Mohammedan emperors.

1381.　Insurrection of Wat Tyler; and upon its suppression by the barons, not fewer than 1500 of the insurgents were hanged, many of them without trial.

1394.　The followers of Wickliffe, the Reformer, persecuted.

1398.　Tyrannical rule of Richard II. Rebellion in Ireland, on account of the "Kilkenny Statutes" passed in 1367. These Statutes declared alliance of the English settlers

* 'Interestihg Historical Events,' Part I., p. 198.

by marriage with the "mere Irish" to be *high treason;* for wearing the Irish clothing and adopting their customs, the penalty was *confiscation of property* or *imprisonment;* submission to the Breton law was construed to be treason; suffering the Irish to graze their cattle upon the lands of the "Pale," presenting Irishmen to benefices, admitting them to monasteries, entertaining their bards, etc., were made *penal;* while to tax an Englishman was declared *felony.*

1399. Forced abdication and subsequent murder of Richard II. by Bolingbroke, who usurped the crown under the title of Henry IV., to the exclusion of the two rightful heirs, who were confined in Windsor Castle.

1410. John Badby burnt at Smithfield for heresy, the Prince of Wales (afterwards Henry V.) being present. About the time of Henry IV. severe tortures were thus applied:—"The man or woman shall be remanded to the prison, and laid there in some low and dark house, where they shall lie naked on the bare earth, without any litter, rushes or other clothing, and without any garments about them . . . . and that they shall lie upon their backs, their heads uncovered, and their feet and one arm shall be drawn to one quarter of the house with a cord, etc., the other arm to another quarter; and in the same manner shall be done with their legs; and there shall be laid upon their bodies iron and stone, so much as they may bear and more; and the next day following they shall have three morsels of barley bread without any drink; and the second day they shall drink thrice of the water that is next to the house of the prison (except running water), without any bread; and this shall be their diet until they be dead." This horrible torture continued to be legal down to the time of George III. The date at which it was last inflicted has not been ascertained, but certainly it was the recognised mode by which prisoners charged with felony were compelled to put themselves on their trial, by pleading either guilty or not guilty. Mr. Barrington, in his 'Ancient Statutes,' p. 86, mentions two instances which happened in the reign of George II., in the year 1741.*

From the year 1468 until the Commonwealth, the practice of torture was frequent, and many instances of it are recorded in the Council books, and the torture warrants in many cases are still in existence. The last instance on record occurred in 1640, when one Archer, a glover, who was supposed to have been concerned in the riotous attack upon Archbishop Laud's palace at Lambeth, "was racked in the Tower," as a contemporary letter states, "to make him confess his companions." A copy of the warrant, under the Privy Seal, authorising the torture in this case, is in the State Paper Office. James II., when in Scotland, had been present during the infliction of torture.

1413. Laws enacted for the extirpation of heresy.

1415. John Claydon and Richard Turman burnt at Smithfield for heresy.

1441. Eleanor Cobham, Duchess of Gloucester; the astronomer Roger Bolingbroke, Canon Southwell, Margery Jourdayne and John Hum, condemned for witchcraft. The Duchess was banished; Bolingbroke hanged, drawn and quartered; Margery Jourdayne burnt, Southwell died in prison, and Hum was pardoned.

1455. Commencement of the civil wars of "The Roses" between the Lancastrians (who chose the *red rose* as their symbol) and the Yorkists (who chose the *white* one). These wars terminated in 1485, and in them perished 12 princes of the blood royal, 200 nobles, and 100,000 gentry and common people. Almost the whole country was depopulated, and its aristocracy exterminated.

1478. Conviction and execution of witches.

* See the article 'Peine Forte et Dure,' in the 'Political Cyclopedia,' vol. iv. p. 500.

1483. Usurpation of Richard III.; murder of his young nephews King Edward V. and the Duke of York in the Tower of London, and of Lord Rivers and others in Pomfret Castle.

1485. Accession of Henry VII. Immense sums accumulated by extortion and confiscations enabled him to rule without the assistance or control of Parliament. He revived the arbitrary taxes known by the ironical name of *benevolences*.

1509. Accession of Henry VIII., a tyrant who boasted "that he never spared man in his rage, or woman in his lust." During his reign, the royal prerogative attained its greatest height. The creation of new and 'unheard of treasons also characterized it.

1532. Punishment of *boiling to death* inflicted upon a man convicted of poisoning seventeen persons.

1534. Execution of the "Holy Maid of Kent;" two persons burnt at Smithfield for heresy.

1535. Nine clergymen, who refused to admit the spiritual supremacy of Henry, hanged and quartered at Tyburn. Archbishop Fisher and Sir Thomas More (the Chancellor) beheaded for the same reason. Universal horror produced on the Continent by these atrocities.

1536. Anne Boleyn beheaded; Henry marries Jane Seymour.

1537. The revenues of 193 monasteries, amounting to £2,653,000. confiscated to the crown. The abbey lands partitioned among Henry's courtiers.

1538. Two baptists burnt for heresy.

1539. The abbots of Reading, Glastonbury and Colchester for denying the king's supremacy were hanged and quartered. Publication of the "Bloody Statute," or "Six articles in support of the papal doctrines of transubstantiation," &c., &c. Persecution of Reformers in Scotland— seven burnt for heresy. The king's proclamations voted by

Parliament to have the force of law. Total dissolution of religious houses in England and Wales—643 monasteries, 90 colleges, 2374 churches and free chapels, and 100 hospitals. The immediate consequence of this measure was that large numbers of their inmates became outcasts and wanderers, as did also the poor who had been employed or supported by those establishments.

1540. The order of knights Hospitallers dissolved, and their property seized by the king. Henry marries Anne of Cleves, Jane Seymour having died in 1537; but separated from her after living with her only six months, and then married Catherine Howard.

1541. The venerable Countess of Salisbury, Margaret, daughter of George, Duke of Clarence and the last of the Plantagenets, beheaded May 27. She refused to lay her head on the block, scorning to die as a criminal, not being conscious of any crime. The executioner pursued her round and round the scaffold, aiming at her hoary head, which he at last struck off, after mangling the neck and shoulders in the most horrible manner.

1542. Catherine Howard beheaded.

1543. Sixth marriage of Henry with Catherine Parr who survived him.

1546. Torture and execution of Anne Ascue for heresy; three men being burned with her for rejecting transubstantiation.

1547. Death of Henry VIII., Jan. 28, aged 56. No English sovereign ever exercised a more despotic authority over his people. Accession of Edward VI.

1549. Beggary and misery throughout the land (See 1539). Laws of the utmost severity passed. Justices empowered to order the letter V. (for *vagabond*) to be branded or burnt upon any vagrant's breast, and adjudge him to serve the informer for two years *as his slave.* Formidable rebellion in Norfolk.

1553. Accession of Mary, who re-establishes popery.

1554. Execution of Lady Jane Grey and Lord Guildford Dudley, February 12.

1555. Persecution of Protestants. Bishops Ridley and Latimer burnt at Oxford as obstinate heretics. The prisons are crowded with heretics. Mary resigns the Church lands and tithes "as essential to her salvation." Crimes greatly increase; highway robberies and disgusting offences abound; fifty criminals hanged at one assizes at Oxford; men of rank become robbers.

1558. Death of Queen Mary, November 17, aged 42. During this Queen's short reign of five years, 285 persons were burned alive—including 5 bishops, 21 clergymen, 56 women and 4 children, while thousands suffered, for conscience sake, the loss of goods, liberty and health.

Accession of Queen Elizabeth, who forbids the elevation of the host in the Chapel Royal. Persecution and burning of Roman Catholics for refusing to deny the Pope's power to depose the Queen. The multitude of monopolies a great cause of complaint.

1586. Trial of Mary Queen of Scots at Fotheringay Castle, on a charge of participating in Babington's conspiracy against Elizabeth. She had been reduced, by the rigour of eighteen years' confinement, from a healthy and beautiful young woman to a sickly cripple.

1587. Mary Queen of Scots beheaded, February 8, aged 44.

1588. Dreadful severities towards Irish Catholics.

1601. Death of Queen Elizabeth, March 24th, aged 70. Accession of James I. (VI. of Scotland and son of Mary Queen of Scots). Declaration against religious toleration. Emigration of Puritans to America.

1604. James endeavours to suppress Presbyterianism in Scotland: 10 leaders imprisoned, 300 clergymen ejected. Other persecutions follow. Laws against witchcraft and witches. In 1603 James published the third edition of his work upon Demonology, in which he gives a very formal account of the practices and illusion of evil spirits, the compacts of witches, the ceremonies used by them, the manner of detecting them, and the justice of punishing them.*

Parliament passed a statute every clause of which is in accordance with this work, and such was its servile subserviency and toadyism to that monarch that it was acted upon and enforced with the severest vigilance ; so much so that from his accession to the latter end of the 17th century, however incredible it may appear, the enormous number of three thousand, one hundred and ninety-two individuals were condemned and executed in Great Britain alone under the accusation of witchcraft, sorcery or conjuration.† Amongst these victims were two widows sentenced to be hanged by Chief Justice Hale, on the mere evidence of their enemies for having bewitched three children, who were too ill to appear in court, but next day called upon the Judge, in perfect health, having been restored at the *very moment conviction was pronounced.*

1625. Death of James I, aged 69. He is succeeded by Charles I, his son. Forced loans, arbitrary taxation, and imprisonments produce the greatest discontent.

* And yet of this royal pedant, called the wisest fool in Christendom, and who, as Macaulay says, was placed on the throne by Providence, in order to show the world what a king ought *not* to be, the then Archbishop of Canterbury, declared that " *undoubtedly His Majesty spoke by the special assistance of God's spirit.*"

† Mackinnon's ' History of Civilisation,' vol. ii. p. 310. " The chief promoters of the accusations for sorcery at this time," says the above author, " were James VI. of Scotland, Pope Innocent X., Sprenger, Bodenus, and Matthew Stephens—a worthy confraternity !" About the same time (that is, in 1601) the Inquisition in Portugal actually condemned to death and burned alive the horse of an Englishman which performed those docile feats this noble animal can be trained to, alleging that it was through diabolical aid.

1629.　The power of the " Star Chamber "* enforced.

The four following instances will suffice to give some idea of the atrocious proceedings of this miscalled court of justice. Prynne, a barrister, having written a book obnoxious to the Court party, was condemned to be expelled the bar, to stand in the pillory at Westminster and Cheapside, and to lose both ears, one in each of those places, to pay a fine of £5000. to the King, and to perpetual imprisonment.

Colonel Lilburne, being accused of writing and disseminating seditious pamphlets, was ordered to be examined, but refused to take the oath used in the Star Chamber, namely, that he would answer interrogatories although his replies might criminate himself. For this contempt of Court, as it was called, he was sentenced to be whipped, pilloried, and imprisoned; and as, while undergoing flagellation, he declaimed loudly against the tyranny of the Government, the Star Chamber, then sitting, ordered him to be gagged.

Williams, the learned Bishop of Lincoln, whose popular preaching marked him for the vengeance of Laud, Archbishop of Canterbury, was, for no other reason, fined £10,000., committed to the Tower during the King's pleasure, and suspended from his episcopal duties. Nor was this all, for during the seizure of his furniture and books there having been found some letters addressed to him by one Osbaldistone, a schoolmaster, another fine of £8000. was levied upon him, while the poor pedagogue, being brought to trial, was sentenced to pay a fine of £5000., and to have his ears nailed to the pillory before his own school.

---

* So called from the *Starra*, or Jewish covenants, deposited there in the reign of Richard I. No *star* was allowed to be valid except found in these repositories. The court was instituted 2 Henry VII. 1487 for trials by a committee of the Privy Council. In Charles I.'s reign it exercised its power independent of any law. There were from 26 to 42 judges. It was abolished 16 Charles I. 1641.

I

1641. Rebellion in Ireland and massacre of 40,000 Protestants.

1642. Commencement of the civil war.

1649. Charles, arraigned as a "tyrant, traitor, murderer, and public enemy to the Commonwealth," was found guilty January 12, and beheaded at Whitehall on January 30. The Commonwealth proclaimed.

1656. Cromwell inaugurated as *Lord Protector*, at Westminster Hall June 26. Severity of his government; men executed without legal trial; many prisoners taken in war, together with fifty gentlemen, who were disaffected to the existing Government, were transported to Barbadoes, there to be sold as *slaves*. The decimation of the Royalists was made to extend to all who had ever avowed themselves of the King's party. The country was parcelled out into military districts, each under the command of a major-general, with authority to arrest and imprison all dangerous and suspected persons.

But, passing on to more recent times, let us now consider what was our own conduct in India after we became possessed of power there.

Referring to the occurrences subsequent to our deposing Meer Cossim from the government of Bengal, " I can only say," writes Clive, " that such a scene of anarchy, corruption, and extortion was never seen or heard of in any country but Bengal ; the three provinces of Bengal, Behar and Orissa, producing a revenue of £3,000,000. sterling, have been under the absolute management of the Company's servants ever since Meer Jaffier's restoration to the Soubahship; and they have, both civil and military, exacted and levied contributions from every man of power and consequence from the Nabob down to the lowest Zemindar. The trade has been carried on by free merchants acting as gomastahs to the Company's servants, who, under the sanction of their names, have committed actions *which make*

*the name of the English stink in the nostrils of a Gentoo and
a Mussulman;* and the Company's servants have interfered
with the revenues of the Nabob, and turned out and put in
officers of the Government at their pleasure, and made
every one pay for their preferment."*

A severe famine followed upon this misgovernment, so
that it is not surprising to find the Governor-General, Lord
Cornwallis, twenty years afterwards, describing Bengal as a
country that was hastening to decay. These are his words:
" I am sorry to be obliged to say that agriculture and commerce have, for many years, been gradually declining, and
that, at present, excepting the class of Sheefs and Ban-
yans, who reside almost entirely in great towns, the inhabitants of these provinces are advancing hastily to a
general state of poverty and wretchedness. In this description I must even include almost every Zemindar in the
Company's territories; which, though it may have been
partly occasioned by their own indolence and extravagance,
I am afraid must also be in a great measure attributed to
the defects of our former system of mismanagement."†

Nor was it in our own territory alone that the evil of our
misrule was felt. It spread into the dominions of our allies.
From our first connection with the Nabob of Oude, his
principality was made a carcass for the British to prey upon.
" I fear," said Mr. Hastings, when still vested with the
supreme rule over India, and describing a state of things
which he himself had been a party in producing, " I fear
that our *encroaching spirit, and the insolence with which it
has been exerted, has caused our alliance to be as much
dreaded by all the powers of Hindostan as our arms. Our
encroaching spirit and the uncontrolled and even protected
licentiousness of individuals have done more injury to our
national reputation than our arms and the credit of our
strength has raised it.* Every person in India dreads a

---

* See Macaulay's ' Essay on Lord Clive.'   † See Correspondence.

connection with us, which they see attended with mortifying humiliation to those who have availed themselves of it."* And as a signal example of this feeling, and of measures which awakened it, he adduces our dealings with Oude.

"Before those dealings commenced, Oude," says the historian Mill, "was in a high state of prosperity; it yielded, without pressure upon the people, a clear income of three millions, but by 'quartering, not only an army of soldiers, but a host of civilians upon him, we soon reduced the Nabob to a state of the bitterest distress and his country to poverty; so that, after bearing the burthen for some years, he found his income reduced to half its former amount. In nine years, unjustifiable extortions, to the amount of thirty-four lacs of rupees (£340,000.) per annum had been practised in that dependent province."† "The numbers, influence and enormous amount of the salaries, pensions and encroachments of the Company's service, civil and military, in the Vizier's service," said Mr. Hastings, "have become an intolerable burthen upon the revenue and authority of his Excellency, and exposed us to the enmity and resentment of the whole country, by excluding the native servants and adherents of the Vizier from the rewards of their services and attachment. I am afraid that few men would understand me if I were to ask by what right or policy we levied a tax on the Nabob Vizier for the benefit of patronized individuals, and fewer still if I questioned the right or policy of imposing upon him an army for his protection, which he could not pay and which he does not want; with what expression of features could I tell him to his face 'You do not want it, but you shall pay for it.'"‡

Mr. Hastings did not content himself with this exposure

---

* Gleig's 'Life of Warren Hastings,' vol. ii.
† Mill's 'History of India,' vol. v. p. 316.
‡ 'Life of Warren Hastings,' vol. ii. p. 458.

of events which had occurred under his own administration. He withdrew a portion of that army which the Nabob " did not want, but for which he was obliged to pay ;" but this burthen was fastened upon him again with additions by Mr. Hastings' successor, Lord Cornwallis, in spite of the Nabob's earnest deprecations. Having gradually increased our demands under the name of subsidy from £250,000. to £700,000. per annum, Lord Teignmouth (Sir John Shore) further increased it, and Lord Wellesley, under a threat of seizing upon the whole, in 1801, extorted a surrender from the Nabob of one-half of his dominions, valued at £1,300,000. of annual revenue, in satisfaction of a demand which he had imposed upon him of £700,000. But our exactions did not stop here; between the years 1815 and 1825 were extracted more than four millions under the name of loans from the Nabob, or, " as they might be more justly described," says the Governor-General Lord Bentinck, " as unwilling contributions extorted for fear of our power, for which we gave him the empty title of King, and a territory entirely unproductive, little better than a wilderness."

A short digression will here be necessary to complete the story of British injustice to Oude.

The climax to the wrongs of Oude was its annexation by Lord Dalhousie in open violation of the treaty of 1837, which he scrupled not to declare " was null and void, having been wholly disallowed by the Honourable Court of Directors as soon as they received it." And this in defiance of the facts—that the treaty bore the signatures of the then Governor-General Lord Auckland and three members of the Council in the usual form ; that it had been formally referred to as a subsisting treaty in two separate communications from the Governor-General to the King of Oude in the years 1839 and 1847; and lastly that it was included in a volume which was published in 1845 by the authority of Government. (See Oude Blue Book.)

The case having been submitted in 1857 to the eminent jurist, Dr. Travers Twiss, for his opinion, that learned gentleman gave it as follows :

" Upon the best consideration which I have been able to give to all these facts, I am constrained to come to the conclusion that the Governor-General of India in Council was not authorised by the law of nations to set aside the treaty of 1837 as inoperative."

And yet, notwithstanding this opinion of so eminent an authority, a recent writer who appears to have about as much respect for the Decalogue as for the Law of Nations, scruples not to defend the annexation of Oude, by the *stet pro ratione voluntas* argument, an argument which would equally justify the thus ennobled art of kleptomania whether practised by the bold brigand or the sneaking pickpocket. " There was still," says Mr. Kaye * another province to be absorbed into the British Empire, under the administration of Lord Dalhousie ; not by conquest, for its rulers had ever been our friends and its people had recruited our armies ; not by lapse, for there had always been a son or a brother, or some member of the royal house to fulfil, according to the Mohammedan law of succession, the conditions of heirship, and there was still a king, the son of a king, upon the throne ; *but by the simple assertion of the dominant will of the British Government*. This was the great province of Oude, in the very heart of Hindostan, *which had long tempted us alike by its local situation and the reputed wealth of its natural resources*." Hear this, ye venerable shades of Grotius, Puffendorf and Vattel ! Read this, ye *so-called independent princes of India, and* meditate thereon !

Lord Cornwallis was indisputably a just man, Lord Teignmouth a religious man, and Lord Wellesley a great man ; nevertheless, there was nothing wise or great, just or

* Kaye's ' History of the Sepoy War in India,' vol. i. p. 112.

religious in their treatment of their helpless allies, the sovereign princes of Oude.

Mr. Dundas, afterwards Lord Melville, bears like testimony against our treatment of native Indian princes. In a speech delivered by him in the House of Commons on April 15th, 1782, he said:

"There were four principal conterminous powers in India—the Mahratta states; the dominions of Hyder Ali; the dominions of the Nizam of the Deccan, and the dominions of the Rajah of Berar. Besides these, there were several inferior powers, such as the Nabob of Arcot, the Rajah of Tanjore, etc. But the four principal powers had all been inflamed against us, with two of whom we were at open war and the other two were justly incensed against us. The Presidency of Bombay entered into a negotiation with Ragoba, a person who had pretensions to be a ruler of the Mahrattas states, promising to seat him in the Government, if he would give up, when so seated, certain territories to the Company. With this treaty they entered upon the war, and soon after, the Presidency of Bengal formed a treaty of exactly the same kind with Moodegee Benslah, the Rajah of Berar, offering to seat him in the Government of the Mahrattas, if he would cede certain districts. This double dealing was discovered, and Moodegee Benslah resented it as insidious and unfaithful. The Nizam of the Deccan's dominions lay to the north of our possessions, and they were so obnoxious to them that we ought to be very careful in our treatment of him. He ceded to the Company certain districts, which were to be paid for by an annual tribute. The tribute we failed to pay. The consequence was that he declared the British to be a nation which no promises could bind, and no rules of justice, honour or faith could restrain; and he invited the power of Hyder Ali against us; for no Indian was safe while the English had an inch of territory in India."

After the above instances, recorded by Englishmen themselves, of British bad faith and misrule in India, the opinions
and sentiments expressed in the following State Paper, delivered to Sir Robert Ainslie, the English ambassador at
Constantinople, by the Grand Vizier, will appear neither
surprising nor unjust.   The document in question was
read by Mr. Grey, M.P., in the House of Commons,
on the 29th Feb., 1792, during the debate on the Russian
armament.

Towards the close of his speech, Mr. Grey said : " Those
allies, the Turks, whom we pretended to support, but
afterwards betrayed, had given the highest proof of their
abhorrence and contempt of our conduct. I know not
whether I shall be blamed or ridiculed for what I have done,
but I have taken the pains to procure the best information
on the subject, and have obtained a copy of the Grand
Vizier's answer to Sir Robert Ainslie, our ambassador at
Constantinople, of which the following is the substance :*—

STATE PAPER.

" The Grand Seignior wars for himself, and for himself
makes peace. He can trust his own slaves, servants, and
subjects.   He knows their faith, has experienced their
virtue, and can rely upon their fidelity—a virtue long since
banished your corner of Europe. *If all other Christians tell
truth,* no reliance is to be had on England; she buys and
sells all mankind. The Ottomans have no connexion with
your King nor your country ; we never sought for your
advice, your interference, or your friendship ; we have no
minister, no agency, no correspondence with you; for what
reason offer you then to mediate for us with Russia ?   Why
seek ye to serve an empire of Infidels, as ye call us Mussul-
men ? We want not your friendship, aid, or mediation.

* ' Parliamentary History,' vol. xxix., p. 933. See also the *Times* news-
paper of Feb. 29, 1792.

Your Vizier, of whom you speak so highly, must have some project of deception in view, some oppressive scheme to amuse your nation, who, we are told, are credulous, servile, and adorers only of money. AVARICE, if we are well informed, is your chief characteristic; you sell and buy your God—*money is your deity*; and all things is commerce with your ministry, with your nation—come ye, then, to sell us to Russia? No, let us bargain for ourselves. When fate has spun out the thread of our good fortune we must yield; what has been decreed by God and the Prophet of men must and will come to pass. *The Ottomans know no finesse; duplicity and cunning are your Christian morals.* We are not ashamed to be honest, downright, plain, and faithful in our state maxims. If we fall in war, we submit to the will of heaven, decreed from the beginning. We have long lived in splendour, the first power on earth, and we glory in having triumphed for ages over Christian infidelity and depravity, mixed with all sorts of vice and hypocrisy. *We adore the God of nature and believe in Mahomet. You neither believe in the God you pretend to worship, nor in his Son, whom you call both your God and your Prophet.* What reliance can there be upon so sacrilegious a race? Truth you banish, as you do virtue, from all your conduct and actions with each other. Read the catalogue of complaints, manifestoes, declarations, and remonstrances of all the Christian Kings, Monarchs, and Emperors, who have lived and warred with each other. You find them all equally blasphemous, equally perfidious, equally cruel, equally unjust, and *faithless to their engagements.* Did the Turk ever forfeit his promise, word, or honour? Never! *Did ever a Christian Power keep an engagement but while it suited his own avarice or ambition?* No! How, then, do you think we are to trust you, a nation at this moment, if the truth be told, ruled by a perfidious administration, without one grain of virtue to guide the machine of State. The

Grand Seignior has no public intercourse with your court—
he wants none—he wishes for none. If you wish to remain
here as a spy, or, as you term yourself, an ambassador for
your court, you may live with those of other Christian
nations, while you demean yourself with propriety, but we
want neither your aid by sea or land, nor your council or
mediation. I have no order to thank you for your offer,
because it is by the Divan deemed officious, nor have I any
command to thank you for the offer of your naval assistance,
because it is what the Porte never dreamed of admitting
into our sea. What you have to do with Russia we neither
know nor care; our concerns with that court we mean to
finish as suits ourselves and the maxims of our laws and
State policy. *If you are not* the most profligate Christian
nation, as you are charged to be, you are undoubtedly the
boldest in presumption and effrontery, in offering to bring
such a power as Russia to terms. Such as you and some
other trivial Christians united fancy yourselves equal to
command; we know better, and therefore this effrontery of
yours amounts rather to audacity, and to an imbecile dicta-
tion, which must render your councils at home mean and
contemptible, and your advice abroad unworthy of wisdom
or attention from any power, much less the regard of the
Porte, which on all occasions wherein its ministers have
listened to you have experienced evil either in your designs
or in your ignorance.

"His Sublime Highness cannot be too much upon his
guard against the attempts and presumption of a nation so
perfidious to the interests of its subjects (or colonists), but
it is the usual way of Christian Princes to sell and cede over
their subjects to each other for money. *Every peace made
amongst you,* as we are well informed, is made favourable to
the King that best bribes. The Ottoman Ministry have too
long and too often given ear to European councils, and as
often as they did so they either were betrayed, sold, or

deceived. Away, then, with your interference for the Porte with Russia. *It has been your aim* to embroil all mankind, and thereafter profit by your perfidy. We ask not, want not, nor desire your commerce, because our merchants have been sacrificed to your double dealings. *You have no religion* but gain; avarice is your only God, and the Christian faith you profess but as a mask for your hypocrisy. We will hear no more from you, therefore you are commandèd to make no reply."

With the view of proving how powerful and beneficial an influence the doctrines of the Koran exert over the feelings and actions of the Mohammedans, we shall conclude the present chapter with a few extracts from a work entitled 'La Turquie Actuelle,' written by A. Ubbicini, and published by him in 1855 :—

TRUTHFULNESS AND HONESTY.

" The aspect of these vast galleries (bazaars), presenting an assemblage of all the nations and all the industries of Turkey, offers an opportunity of adding some features to the physiognomy of the Osmanli or Turk. See him there gravely seated on the front of his stall, beside his Armenian or Greek fellow-tradesmen ; whilst they watch with the eye the passing customer, and invite him with the voice—' Hola hé ! Captain ! Ichlébi ! Signor Captain !'—he continues quietly to smoke his pipe or to pass the beads of his chapter. If you stop before his berth and ask him the price of an object, he will answer politely but laconically, ' Fifty—a hundred piastres.' If unaccustomed to the habits of the place, you commence to bargain, his only answer will be a gentle raising of the chin and a resumption of his pipe. In vain will you insist, he will not lower his price a para. It is quite otherwise with the Christians and the Jews.

From the hundred piastres they will come down to eighty, to sixty, to forty, or even below.

" As a general rule, offer to an Armenian the half of the price he asks, the third to a Greek, the fourth to a Jew. But for the Mussulman, if you want to get his goods, resign yourself at once to pay what he asks for them.

" *As no one could make an Osmanli* break his word*, he believes implicitly in the word of others. Make an oath that such a thing is true, he will believe you. A French officer went to the bazaar to buy a piece of cloth, and asked for the same his comrade had bought the day before; but the merchant had no more of it. He went to another who asked a higher price. The officer complained and showed him his pattern. The merchant having examined the pattern, and seen that the quality was the same as that of his own piece, proposed to his customer to make oath as to the price which he had given for his cloth. The officer, anxious to see what the result would be, did so, upon which the merchant gave him the cloth for the same price as the other.

" I confess," says M. Ubbicini, " that this confidence in a man's word, this dignity and reserve please me. I know not why the seller with us should affect to place himself so much below the buyer. In Turkey there is no such distinction. In fact, the seller troubles himself little about his sale, and sees, without jealousy, the greater success of his neighbour. ' My turn will come to-morrow,' he says. When the voice of the Muezin is heard, he performs his prayers and prosternations in his shop, in the middle of all the comers and goers, as little disturbed as if he were in the Desert; or he goes to the neighbouring mosque, leaving his merchandise under the guardianship of the public faith.

* The Persians call the Turks Osmanlis, because they assert "that Osman or Othman was the true and lawful successor of Mohammed, the great Caliph and lawful sovereign, to whom alone belonged the interpretation of the Koran, and the deciding the difficulties which arise in the law."

In this immense capital (Constantinople), where the merchants are accustomed to absent themselves from their shops at fixed hours, known to every one, where the doors of houses are only shut at night, by a simple latch, *there are not four robberies committed in the whole year.* At Pera and Galata, exclusively inhabited by Christians, there is not a day passes without hearing of robberies and murders.

There is the same honesty to be found in the country parts; here is the narrative of an English traveller, in a letter lately addressed to the *Daily News* :—

" Yesterday, I hired a Bulgarian peasant, with his waggon, to carry my baggage and that of my companion, consisting of trunks, portmanteaus, carpet-bags, cloaks, furs and shawls. Wishing to buy some hay to stretch ourselves on during the night, a Turk, polite, if ever a man was, offered to accompany us. The peasant unyoked his oxen, and left them with all our baggage in the street. When I saw that he was also going away, I said, ' Some one must remain here.' ' Why ?' asked the Turk, with surprise. ' To watch over my goods.' ' Oh !' replied the Mussulman, ' they may remain here all the week, night and day, and no one will touch them.' I yielded, and when I returned, I found all safe. Observe that the Turkish soldiery were continually passing the spot. Let this be told to the Christians from the pulpits of London. Some will think that they dream. Let them awake." . . . .

The honesty of the porters (hammals) is even more to be depended upon than that of our Auvergnats. It is they who carry the bales of spices from the counting-houses of Galata to the vessels, and *vice versâ ;* and I believe there is not a single example of one packet being wanting. It is true, this is rendered more easy by the proverbial honesty of the whole nation.

A merchant of Galata was returning to Constantinople

with a sack of two thousand piasters in *bechlics*—pieces of five piasters—while disembarking at the landing-place at Topkhané, the sack bursts, the pieces fall out and are scattered on the quay; some of them roll into the sea. The crowd throws itself on the pavement; some plunge into the water. The alarmed owner follows all these movements; he begins to be reassurred as he sees that from all sides the piasters as they are found are replaced in the sack. A *hammal* then takes up the sack on his shoulders and accompanies the merchant to his house. The latter having paid the hammal for his job, hastens to count his bechlics; not one was missing.

Toleration and Charity.

Our negligence in observing the precepts of our religion, the human considerations that interfere with its most essential parts, the facility with which we abandon it for the most miserable motives, are taken by the Turks as so many proofs of the inferiority of this religion. It is on that account they call Europe "the land of the infidels," and that in speaking of us they join the epithet *Mulhed* (impious) to that of *Ghaiour* (infidel).

But this contempt does not lead to persecution. I have elsewhere shown on the authority of many examples how the spirit of proselytism and intolerance of which the Turks are often accused, is not only contrary to the principle, but to the constant practice of Islamism. As nothing in the world can cause an Osmanli to renounce his religion, so he never seeks to disturb the faith of another. If you please him, and if you have attracted his affection, he may say to you, "God grant to thee a happy end," which means, "God give thee grace to become a Mussulman." But that would be all; to go further would be to encroach upon the "divine domain." "The conversion of souls," say the Mussulman doctors, " belongs to God." Here is another maxim of these doctors—" Do good to every one, and dispute not with the ignorant." Turkey has never known religious persecutions; on the contrary, she offers an asylum upon her territory to the unhappy victims of Christian fanaticism. Consult history. In the 15th century, thousands of Israelites, driven out of Spain and Portugal, found a refuge in this same Turkey, where their descendants for four centuries have led a quiet existence, except in those places (must one confess it?) where they had to defend themselves against the persecutions of the Christians, and above all of the orthodox (Catholics). Even to day, at Athens, so long as Easter lasts, a Jew dares not show himself in the streets. In Turkey, if the Israelitish race are exposed to insult from the Greek and Armenian Christians, at least the local authorities interfere to protect them.

All religions, as well as all nationalities, are to be found, side by side, in the vast and pacific dominions of the Sultan. The mosque, it is true, overtops the Church and the Synagogue, but it does not exclude them. Catholicism is freer at Constantinople and at Smyrna, than at Paris and at Lyons. No law restrains its outward manipulations and imprisons God in the sanctuary. The dead when carried to their last resting-place, are followed by a long line of monks, carrying candles and singing psalms. The day of the Fête-Dieu, all the churches of Pera and Galata walk in procession, preceded by the cross and the banner, and escorted by a piquet of soldiers, who oblige the Osmanlis themselves to give way for the procession to pass.

But I shall be told, the Catholics of the East are protected by France and by Austria, as Russia protects the Greeks, and England the Protestants. Well, be it so; but the poor Jews, who protects them? Four or five years ago, a Jewish muleteer was brought before the Pasha of Mussoul, accused of having blasphemed the Prophet, which had excited the whole of the population. When he heard the sacrilegious words imputed to the accused, the Pasha drew back in horror, exclaiming,—" It is impossible that any man could have spoken thus without immediately drawing upon his head the vengeance of God. I cannot, therefore, believe that this muleteer is guilty, and it would be presumptuous in me to punish him whom God has not condescended to chastise."

This is a fine example of tolerance! Yet how many people in France believe, upon the faith of the *Augsburgh Gazette,* and the *Athens Observer,* that in Turkey they every day torture and impale those " dogs of Christians," as they believe on the faith of the writers of dramas and comic-operas, in the handkerchief thrown by the SULTAN to his favorite slave, or in the women sewn up alive in sacks and thrown into the Bosphorus.

The Turkish Government has derogated in practice from its tolerant maxims only when it has seen the spirit of proselytism, under cover of this very toleration, becoming aggressive, and bringing trouble at once into the consciences of men and the affairs of the State. The Lazerists only, who first appeared in Turkey in 1781, have wisely understood their vocation ; thus, their missions which now cover the whole of the Levant, are the only ones which at present bear real fruit. The local authorities, far from hindering them, are the first to encourage them in a zeal which seems to be excited only by benevolence. Was it not a Turk, and that one of the principal functionaries of the Porte, HASSIB EFFENDI, who in 1844, after a visit which he had made to the School of the Sisters of Charity, sent to the Superior a magnificent First Communion robe for the poor pupil who should be judged worthy of that favour.

To do good is to the Osmanlis, the first of obligations.— " Let thy door be always open to the dervish and the

poor," said the poet NABI in his *advice to his son*; "to do
this is more agreeable to God than to build mosques, than
to fast continually, or to make many times pilgrimages to
Mecca." With them charity is not distinct from religion.
He who fails to give alms does not merely neglect his duty
as a Mussulman, he ceases by that alone to be one; for
charity, as well as the pilgrimage, the fast of the Ramazan
and prayer, form, with the profession of Faith, the five
fundamental points of Islamism.

I have elsewhere spoken of "that charity and benevolence universal, unlimited, to be exercised, without distinction of belief, or even of personal hatred and animosities,
going even to the exhaustion of private resources, as TACITUS
says of the ancient Germans; and that, not merely in the
towns, but even over the whole of the public roads, where
public and private beneficence has provided for the protection and support of the traveller and the indigent, not
in respect to one's neighbours only, but even to the
animals."

In the passage above referred to, M. Ubicini, after describing the stray dogs in Constantinople, says, "Hunted
away by the Europeans, great numbers have retreated into
the remotest quarters of the city. There they still find some
charitable souls who distribute food to them every morning,
assist the females when whelping, save the puppies from
perishing with cold during the winter, and even carry their
humanity so far as, in their last moments, to bequeath them
a legacy for their support. It is true that the dog, like the
pig, is considered by the Osmanlis as an unclean animal, so
much as to violate by its presence, the state of legal purity.
The dog is therefore never suffered in the house, but the
owner of the latter regards himself as the natural protector
of all such as have domiciliated themselves in the quarter
he inhabits. Benevolence is commanded by the Prophet,

K

as the first of all virtues ; a benevolence which is extended
to all animals.*

"To sum up, in one word, *I know no people more humane,
in the true sense of the word, than those Turks whom we still
to-day continue to treat as Barbarians.*"

* 'La Turquie Actuelle,' p. 78. "To all the brute creation," writes Miss
Pardoe ('City of the Sultan') the Turks are not only merciful, but minis-
tering friends ; and to so great an extent do they carry this kindness towards
the inferior animals that they will not kill an unweaned lamb, in order to
spare unnecessary suffering to the mother ; and an English sportsman, who
had been unsuccessful in the chase, having on one occasion, in firing off his
piece previously to disembarking from his caique, brought down a gull that
was sailing above his head, was reproached by his rowers with as much
horror and emphasis as though he had been guilty of homicide."

PART III.

CHARGES REFUTED.

CHARGES REFUTED.

—◆—

SOLE CHAPTER.

THE charges brought against Mohammed are reducible to four, as follows :—

I. The promulgating a new and false religion as a revelation from God, it being, on the contrary, but a mere invention of his own, for the purpose of gratifying his ambition and lust.

II. That Mohammed propagated his religion by the sword, thereby causing an enormous waste of human blood, and a vast amount of human misery.

III. The sensual character of his Paradise as described in the Koran.

IV. The encouragement he has given to licentiousness by legalizing Polygamy.

We proceed to rebut the above charges, to the best of our ability.

CHARGE I.

The promulgating a new and false religion as a revelation from God, it being, on the contrary, but a mere invention of his own for the purpose of gratifying his ambition and lust.

That Mohammed was wholly free from the vice of ambition, is proved by almost every circumstance of his life, but more especially by the indisputable fact that, after living to see his religion fully established, and himself in possession of unlimited power, he never availed himself of it for the purposes of self-aggrandizement, but retained to the very last his original simplicity of manners.* As to his gratifying his appetite for women, considering that when he appeared, unbounded polygamy obtained throughout Arabia, it must certainly seem somewhat paradoxical that he should restrict licentiousness, the better to satisfy his own lust.

In addition to what has been before observed upon this point,† it may be further urged in Mohammed's defence, that, like all his countrymen, he was, by temperament, an ardent lover of the fair sex; that he never affected to be exempt from human frailties, saying, on the contrary, " I am a man like unto you,‡ and that in comparison with David the prophet and king, " the man after God's own heart," he " was as pure as is the icicle that hangs on Dian's temple." Michal, Saul's second daughter, was David's first wife. She was taken from him during his disgrace ;§ he married successively several others,‖ and still continued to demand back the first. Before she could be restored to him, she had to be forced from a husband who loved her exceedingly, and who followed her as far as he could, crying like a child.¶ David did not scruple to match with a daughter of an uncircumcised prince,** and though he had children by several wives, yet he took concubines at Jerusalem—and lastly, in the case of Bathsheba,†† he added to the sin of adultery, the crime of a deliberate and cold-blooded murder.

When David, by reason of old age, could not be warmed by all the clothes they covered him with, it was thought

---

* See Life, p. 53..
† Page 26.
‡ Koran, chap. xli.
§ 1 Samuel, chap. xxv. 46.

‖ 2 Samuel, chap. iii. v.
¶ 2 Samuel, chap. iii. 16.
** Talmai, King of Geshur, ibid., v. 3.
†† 1 Kings, chap. i.

proper to seek for a young virgin, who might take care of him and lie with him. He suffered them to bring him the most beautiful girl they could find. Now, can this be said to be the action of a very chaste man ? Surely the Christian writers, when they upbraid Mohammed with incontinence, should recollect the saying "that those who live in glass houses should not be the first to throw stones."

In acquiring and using power, Mohammed did but follow the example of Moses, who could not have effected the deliverance of the children of Israel out of Egypt, had he not assumed the authority of a leader and a head—the maker or dispenser of the laws ; and surely no man ever yet upbraided him with making ambition the end and design of that achievement, since without that power he could not have accomplished the mission upon which he had been sent by Jehovah. And thus it was in the case of Arabia, which, being divided into many tribes, frequently at war with one another, Mohammed had no other way of uniting them into one body, and of establishing his religion among them, than by making himself their head or leader, a circumstance which fully exonerates him from the charge of personal ambition.

As to the term imposture, meaning falsehood or forgery, which has been so unsparingly bestowed upon Mohammed's doctrine, the fact that his first principle was the *unity of the Godhead*—a principle preached by Jesus Christ himself— sufficiently shows its injustice. The word—imposture, however, may be meant to apply to his pretension of being a prophet. Now, it is certain that the abolishing of idolatry and the setting up of the worship of the one true God, among a people lost in the first, and ignorant of the latter, was an errand worthy of a mission from heaven. It is also certain that Mohammed did establish the worship of one God in Arabia, and so effectually abolished idolatry in that country, that it has never re-appeared there, in any shape, for above one thousand years, whereas idolatry no sooner got footing again among the Christians, than that section of them that had gained the ascendancy condemned the Iconoclasts as heretics, solely for demolishing the idols that had been set up by them.*

Mohammed's precepts, excepting such as enjoin the extirpating of idolatry, wherever his religion prevailed, enforce the practice of the moral duties which have for object the regulating men's actions towards one another, and that these are recommended with wonderful warmth and pertinacity throughout the Koran, is what has been acknowledged by the greatest of his enemies.

Among the many parables and allegories in which, agreeably to the custom of the Arabians who delighted in that way of speaking and writing, not a few of Mohammed's doctrines are wrapped up, none has excited so much the sarcasm and ridicule of Christian writers as " the night journey to heaven."† But surely these critics should have recollected that such a tale or legend is not a whit more incredible, not a whit more preposterous than that of Christ's temptation by the Devil, in the wilderness.

" Again, the devil taketh him (Christ) up into an exceeding high mountain, and sheweth him all the kingdoms of the earth and the glory of them, &c.† The fact is that the "night journey " is an allegory of easy explanation. Thus, Al Barak, which signifies lightning, is *thought*, which moves more swiftly than even the electric fluid, and the ladder of light by which Gabriel and he ascended up to heaven, was—contemplation—by which we pass through all

* Thus the celebrated Irene, Empress of the East, and wife of Leo IV., surnamed the " Iconoclase," having been declared by her husband, before his death, regent of the Empire for their son, Constantine, caused the latter's eyes to be put out ; then ascended the Imperial throne, and convoked the Council of Nicea in 787, by which the worship of images was re-established.

† See ' Life,' p. 26.

‡ Gospel according to St. Matthew, iv. 8.

the heavens up to the throne of God; and the wonderful cock, whose crowing God took delight in hearing, and which man never heard or regarded, was the prayer of the just, and so on with all the rest.

Upon this point, moreover, it may be fairly asked why Mohammed should be denied the benefit of metaphor and allegory, to which most of the Christian theologians are fain to have recourse in order to solve many things in their own system, and escape from that absurdity which other-wise they would be under; as in the story of the prophet who represents the God of truth as consulting with a lying Spirit in order to deceive Ahab.

"And the Lord said, who shall persuade Ahab that he may go up and fall at Ramoth Gilead? And one said, in this manner; and another said, in that manner."

"And there came forth a spirit and stood before the Lord, and said, I will persuade him.

"And the Lord said unto him, Wherewith? And he said, I will go forth, and I will be a lying spirit in the mouth of all his prophets. And He (God) said, Thou shalt persuade him, and prevail also; go forth and do so."* Is not the whole of Solomon's song maintained to be an alle-gory of Christ's love for his Church? Thus again, with respect to the New Testament, the same excuse must be pleaded when Christ says he is a *vine*, a *way*, a *door*, as well as when he says that the Bread and Wine are his *Body* and *Blood*, since from rejecting the metaphor in this case has sprung up a most notorious piece of idolatry (tran-substantiation) among Christians belonging to the Church of Rome, so that it really seems but an equitable request that Mohammedans should be allowed to make use of the same advantage of the allegory and metaphor to solve the difficulties and seeming absurdities which, otherwise their system might be charged with, none of which are so great

* 1 Kings, chap. xxii. 20, 21, 22.

or nearly so dangerous as that which establishes the doctrine whereby it is taught that a piece of bread or a wafer can be changed by certain words pronounced by a priest, though never so stupid, ignorant or wicked, into the God that created the universe.

It has also been objected that Mohammed, while pretending not to deliver any new religion to the Arabians, but only to revive that old one which God had revealed to Abraham, and Abraham had delivered to Ishmael, the founder of their nation, actually did found a new religion, and, consequently, spake that which was false. But, if that only be a new religion which differs from the former in the object of its worship, and the moral duties imposed by it, then, certainly neither that of Moses, nor that of Jesus Christ, nor that of Mohammed, were new religions. That of Moses was no more than the renewal and enforcement by laws of that religion which Adam, Noah, Abraham, Isaac, Jacob and Ishmael professed, and which was to adore the one only God, and Him to love and obey with their whole soul, and to practise those moral duties which the necessity of human society as well as the will of God imposed upon mankind. Thus, Jesus Christ tells us that to love God above all things and our neighbour as ourselves was the whole law and the prophets, that is, that Moses and the prophets taught the Israelites a religion which entirely consisted in the love and adoration of one eternal God, and an extensive love of one another; and hence the doctrine of Jesus Christ himself was not new, but the same that Moses had taught before, with this only difference, that our moral duties to one another were commanded with more force than before, and this admirable and divine rule set down, by which the meanest and most ignorant of mankind might know with almost certainty when he offended against these moral duties and when not, as the precept " do unto others as you would they should do unto you" clearly shows.

At the appearance of Jesus, the Jews inhabiting Judea were extremely corrupt in their morals, and a criminal self-love and egotism having been long spread among them, both priests and people, there was nothing to be found but avarice, rapine, injustice and oppression, for, placing their righteousness in the rigid observance of some ceremonies and formulas of religion, they had entirely lost its real substance. To restore this seems to have been the whole aim, drift and design of the mission of Christ, for to that all his doctrines plainly tend—a consideration sufficient to show that the Christian religion in its foundation was but the renewing of that of Moses. The business of Mohammed was not only to enforce moral doctrines, but also to establish the adoration of one God, for the people among whom it was his lot to be cast were gone vastly astray in both; it was, therefore, his intent to revive the religion of Ishmael the founder of his nation—namely, the worship of one God; and this is enough to prove that Mohammed did but speak the truth when he told the Arabians that he did not preach to them a new religion, but only the ancient one which their forefather Ishmael had proposed many ages before.

Is it possible to conceive, we may ask, that the man who effected such great and lasting reforms in his own country by substituting the worship of the one only true God for the gross and debasing idolatry in which his countrymen had been plunged for ages; who abolished infanticide, prohibited the use of spirituons liquors and games of chance (those sources of moral depravity), who restricted within comparatively narrow limits the unrestrained polygamy which he found in existence and practice—can we, we repeat, conceive so great and zealous a reformer to have been a mere impostor, or that his whole career was one of sheer hypocrisy? Can we imagine that his divine mission was a mere invention of his own of whose falsehood he was conscious throughout? No, surely, nothing but a consciousness of really righteous intentions could have carried Mohammed so steadily and constantly without ever flinching or wavering, without ever betraying himself to his most intimate connections and companions, from his first revelation to Khadijah to his last agony in the arms of Ayesha.

Surely a good and sincere man, full of confidence in his Creator, who makes an immense reform both in faith and practice, is truly a direct instrument in the hands of God, and may be said to have a commission from Him. Why may not Mohammed be recognized, no less than other faithful, though imperfect servants of God, as truly a servant of God, serving him faithfully though imperfectly? Why may it not be believed that he was, in his own age and country, a preacher of truth and righteousness, sent to teach his own people the unity and righteousness of God, to give them civil and moral precepts suited to their condition.

Mohammed, then, was doubtless fully convinced of his own mission, as well as that in the name of God, and in the character of his Apostle he wrought a great, albeit perhaps an imperfect reform, in his own country. Nor was his belief in his own mission ill founded. Through mockery and persecution the Prophet kept unflinchingly his path; no threats, no injuries hinder him from still preaching to his people the unity and the righteousness of God, and exhorting to a far better and purer morality than had ever up to his time been set before them. He claimed no temporal power, no spiritual domination, he asked but for simple toleration, free permission to win men by persuasion into the way of truth. He required that men should do justice and love mercy, and walk humbly before their God, and, as the sanction of all, he taught that there will be a resurrection of the dead as well of the just and the unjust.

Compare Mohammed with his own degenerate followers,

with Timour at Ispahan, and Nadir Shah at Delhi, with the wretches who, in our times, have desolated Chios and Cyprus, and Kassandra. The entry of an Eastern victor is ordinarily the signal for murder and massacre alike of the armed and unarmed, of the innocent and the guilty. Mohammed had his wrongs to avenge, but they are satisfied by a handful of exceptions to a general amnesty, and the majority, even of these, are ultimately forgiven. It is the temple of God desecrated by idols, which he had come to ransom. With the sublime words, *" Truth is come, let falsehood disappear,"* he shivers, in succession, the 360 abominations which were standing erect, in the holy place, and his work once accomplished, he did not, like his victorious namesake, in later times, fix his throne in the city he had won. He reared no palace for his own honour by the side of the temple which he had recovered to the honour of God. The city of his fathers, the metropolis of his race, the shrine of his religion, was again deserted for his humble dwelling among those who had stood by him in the day of trial.

CHARGE II.

That Mohammed propagated his religion by the sword, thereby causing an enormous waste of human blood, and a vast amount of human misery.

Now, even admitting this to have been the case to a certain extent, and granting that numbers of idolators perished for refusing to acknowledge the existence of the one and only true God, it may be replied, that what God has once commanded can never be unjust at any time, and since Christians are bound to believe that God did command the Israelites to exterminate and extirpate the Canaanites for their idolatry, and that Jehovah even worked a miracle in the execution of that command, by causing the sun and moon to stand still, in order to afford the light necessary for enabling Joshua to complete the slaughter of the enemy, they must, if consistent, admit that Mohammed was justified in propagating his doctrines by the same means, for, if they do not, it would be tantamount to affirming that idolatry was more hateful to God then than now; that it was less odious to him in the time of Mohammed than in that of Moses, or in that of the kings of Israel, whose nation, together with themselves, was destroyed for this sin alone.

That Mohammed waged wars is certain, but they differed essentially from those of Moses in not being wars of extermination, because the laudable objects of the former were to unite the Arabian tribes in one empire, to reclaim them from idolatry and instruct them in the worship of the one and only God, the Creator of all things.

Mohammed received generously and with open arms all who would submit to his law; he, indeed, put the obstinate to death, but he ever spared the innocent blood of women, maidens and infants. In short, he strictly commanded his followers never to molest, but to treat as brethren, all who would accept and obey the Koran. Moses, on the contrary, slaughtered whole nations, without offering or accepting any conditions of mercy; an example never followed by Mohammed, although in many instances by Christian Powers, and more especially by the Spaniards in their conquest of Peru and Mexico.* Nowhere throughout the Koran can be found attributed to the Deity commands wholly opposed to all human ideas of justice and mercy, in fact, as the following among many others.

"And Moses said, 'Thus saith the Lord, put, every man,

---

* That the Spaniards thought themselves justified by the Bible, appears by the book which Sepulveda wrote for the express purpose of vindicating them in the murder of twelve millions of Indians, "*by the example of the Israelites towards the people of Canaan.* Las Casas says in his ' Brevissima relacion de la destruccion de las Indias, " I have seen in the islands of St. Domingo and Jamaica, gibbets erected all over the country to hang thirteen Indians at a time *in honour of the thirteen apostles.* I have seen," continues he, " young children thrown to the dogs to be devoured alive."

his sword by his side, and go in and out throughout the camp, *and slay, every man, his brother, and, every man, his companion, and every man, his neighbour.' "*

" Joshua smote all the country and all their kings, *he left none remaining, but utterly destroyed all that breathed, as the Lord God of Israel had commanded.*"†

" Now go (said Samuel to Saul) and smite Amalek and *utterly destroy all that they have, and spare them not, but slay both man and woman, infant and suckling, ox and sheep, camel and ass.*" ‡

" But of the cities of those people which the Lord thy God doth give thee for an inheritance, thou shalt *save alive nothing that breatheth.*

" But *thou shalt utterly destroy them,* namely, the Hittites, the Amorites, the Canaanites, the Hivites, and the Jebusites, as the Lord thy God hath commanded thee."§

In like manner, where is there to be found in Christ's Sermon on the Mount—a discourse which breathes naught but mercy, loving-kindness and peace—the least sanction or authority for the horrible atrocities afterwards perpetrated in his revered name? To whom, then, it may be asked, are they attributable? The answer is easy—to the Emperor Constantine, falsely surnamed the Great.

After the death of Christ, there were two distinct and successive versions of his doctrines, to which the name of Christianity was given; the first, introduced by the authority of the Apostles, Paul and John; ‖ the second by that of Constantine.

This emperor, who, from political motives exclusively, had embraced Christianity, but who, on account of his

---

* Exodus xxxi. 27.   † Joshua x. 40.
‡ 1 Sàmuel xv. 3.   § Deuteronomy xx. 17.

cruelty, has justly been **called a** second Nero,* presided over the famous Council of **Nicea, commonly called Nice,** in A.D. 324, in which the doctrine of **Christ's divinity was,** for the first time, established.

Regarding the ceaseless, bloody and unprofitable religious disputes in which the lives of thousands of Christians were sacrificed and the most unexampled cruelty exercised, by those who ought to have lived like brothers and friends, St. Hilary, who lived at the time—viz., the fourth century— was Bishop of Poictiers, and one of the early "fathers of the Church," expresses his regret, disapproval and condemnation in these words :—

"It is a thing, equally deplorable and dangerous, that there are as many creeds as opinions among men, as many doctrines as inclinations, and as many sources of blasphemy as there are faults among us ; *because we make creeds arbitrarily, and explain them as arbitrarily.* . . . . Every year, nay, every moon, we make new creeds to describe the invisible mysteries. We repent of what we have done, we defend those who repent, we anathematize those whom we defended. We condemn either the doctrine of others in ourselves, or our own in that of others ; and reciprocally tearing one another to pieces, we have been the cause of each other's ruin.†

It was at the Council of Nicea that Constantine invested the priesthood with that power whence flowed the most disastrous consequences, as the following summary will show : the massacres and devastations of nine mad crusades of Christians against unoffending Turks, during nearly two

---

* He drowned his wife in boiling water ; put to death his own son Crispus ; murdered the two husbands of his sisters, Constantia and Anastasia ; murdered his own father-in-law, Maximilian Hercules ; murdered his nephew, the son of his sister Constantia, a boy only twelve years of age, together with some others not so nearly related, among whom was Sopator, a pagan priest, who refused to give him absolution for the murder of his (Constantine's) father-in-law. Such was the first *Christian* emperor !

† See Gibbon 'Decline and Fall,' vol. II. p. 411. Bohn's edition.

hundred years, in which many millions of human beings perished; the massacres of the Anabaptists; the massacres of the Lutherans and Papists, from the Rhine to the extremities of the North; the massacres ordered by Henry VIII. and his daughter Mary; the massacres of St. Bartholomew in France;* and forty years more of other massacres between the time of Francis I. and the entry of Henry IV. into Paris; the massacres of the Inquisition,† which are more execrable still as being judicially committed, to say nothing of the innumerable schisms, and twenty years of popes against popes, bishops against bishops, the poisonings, assassinations, the cruel rapines and insolent pretensions‡ of more than a dozen popes, who far exceeded a Nero or a Caligula in every species of crime, vice and wickedness; and lastly, to conclude this frightful list, the massacre of twelve millions of the inhabitants of the new world, executed Crucifix in hand!

It surely must be confessed that so hideous and almost uninterrupted a chain of religious wars, for fourteen cen-

---

* Above 500 persons of rank, and 10,000 of inferior condition perished in Paris alone, besides many thousands who were slaughtered in the provinces. The then Pope Gregory XIII. not only granted a plenary indulgence to all who were concerned in the massacre, but also ordered public rejoicings to celebrate the event; and high mass was performed with every circumstance of pomp and splendour. Nay, so unblushing was the effrontery of this vicar of Christ (!) that he caused a medal to be struck in honour of the deed, bearing on one side the likeness of himself, and on the other an effigy of the destroying angel, surmounted by the inscription "*Huguenotorum strages*" (the slaughter of the Huguenots).

† According to the estimate of Llorente, who wrote the history of the Inquisition, the aggregate number of victims burnt from 1481 to 1808, was 34,024.

‡ In 1627 Pope Urban VIII. promulgated the famous Bull, "*In cœna Domini*," which excommunicates all who dare to appeal to a future Council against the bulls and briefs of the Pope; all princes who dare to levy taxes without the permission of the Pope; those who make treaties of alliance with Turks and heretics; and those who complain to secular judges against the wrongs and injuries received from the Court of Rome. When, it may be asked, did Mohammed or any of his successors arrogate to themselves so extensive a power as this?

turies, never subsisted but among Christians, and that none of the numerous nations stigmatized as heathen, ever spilled a drop of blood on the score of theological arguments.

" We must," says M. Jurieu, " freely declare the truth. The kings of France planted Christendom in the country of the Frisons and the Saxons, by Mahometan ways, and the like force was made use of to plant it in the North. The same means were employed against the sects of the Waldenses and the Albigenses who had dared to condemn the Popes, and were also used in the New World. From all which, it plainly appears that we can no longer reproach Mahomet for having propagated his religion by force—that is by denying toleration to any other ; for he might argue thus, *ad hominem,* if force be wrong in its own nature, it can never be lawfully made use of; but you have made use of it from the fourth century up to the present time, and yet you pretend you have done nothing in all this, but what is very commendable. You must, therefore, confess that this way or means is not wrong in its own nature; and, consequently, I might lawfully make use of it in the first years of my vocation. For, it would be absurd to pretend that a thing which was very criminal in the first century should become just in the fourth, or that a thing which was just in the fourth century should not be so in the first one. This might be pretended if God had made new laws in the fourth century. The Mahometans, according to the principles of their faith, are required to employ violence to destroy other religions, and yet they tolerate them now, and have done so for many ages. The Christians have no order but to preach and instruct, and yet, time out of mind, they destroy with fire and sword those who are not of their religion."

The tolerant spirit of Mohammedanism, as contrasted with the bigotry and fanaticism of Christianity, is thus admirably shown by the celebrated historian, Gibbon : " The wars of the Mohammedans were sanctified by the Prophet, but among the various precepts and examples of his life, the Caliphs selected the lessons of toleration that might tend to disarm the resistance of the unbelieving. Arabia was the temple and patrimony of the God of Mohammed; but he beheld with less jealousy and affection the other nations of the earth. The polytheists and idolators who were ignorant of his name might be lawfully extirpated, but a wise policy supplied the obligations of justice, and after some acts of intolerant zeal, the Mohammedan conquerors of Hindoostan have spared the pagodas of that devout and populous country. The disciples of Abraham, of Moses and of Jesus were solemnly invited to accept the more perfect revelation of Mohammed; but, if they preferred the payment of a moderate tribute, they were entitled to the freedom of conscience and religious worship. In a field of battle, the forfeit lives of the prisoners were redeemed by the profession of Islamism; the females were bound to embrace the religion of their masters, and a race of sincere proselytes was gradually multiplied by the education of the infant captives. But the millions of African and Asiatic converts who swelled the native bands of the faithful Arabs, must have been allured rather than constrained to declare their belief in *one* God and the Apostle of God. By the repetition of a sentence and the loss of a foreskin, the subject or the slave, the captive or the criminal, arose, in a moment, the free and equal companion of the victorious Moslem. Every sin was expiated, every engagement was dissolved; the vow of celibacy was superseded by the indulgence of nature, the native spirits who slept in the cloister were awakened by the trumpet of the Saracens, and in the convulsions of the world, every member of a new society ascended to the natural level of his capacity and courage."

In proof of the correctness of the view thus taken by the historian of the tolerant **character** of Mohammed, the following public document **is here inserted,** being extracted from a work entitled 'A Description of the East and other Countries,' by Richard Pococke, Bishop of Meath, and published in 1743, vol. i. p. 268. The high character of its author for piety, integrity and learning is a sufficient voucher for the authenticity of the documeut, which is as follows :—

The Patent of Mohammed, which he granted to the Monks of Mount Sinai, and to Christians in general.

" As God is great and governeth, from whom all the prophets are come, for there remaineth no record of injustice against God; through the gifts that are given unto men, Mohammed, the son of Abdallah, the Apostle of God, and careful guardian of the whole world, has written the present instrument, to all those that are his national people, and of his religion, as a secure and positive promise to be accomplished to the Christian nation and relations of the Nazareen, whosoever they may be, whether they be the noble or the vulgar, the honourable or otherwise, saying thus :

I. Whosoever of my nation shall presume to break my promise and oath which is contained in this present agreement, destroys the promise of God, acts contrary to the oath and will be a resister of the faith (which God forbid !) for he becometh worthy of the curse, whether he be the king himself or a poor man, or what person soever he may be.

II. That whenever any of the monks in his travels shall happen to settle on any mountain, hill, village, or in any other habitable place, on the sea or in deserts, or in any convent, church, or house of prayer, I shall be in the midst of them, as the preserver and protector of them, their goods and effects, with my soul, aid and protection, jointly with all my national people, because they are a part of my own people, and an honour to me.

III. Moreover, I command all officers not to require any

poll tax of them or any other tribute, because they shall not be forced or compelled to anything of this kind.

IV. None shall presume to change their judges or governors, but they shall remain in their office without being deposed.

V. No one shall molest them when they are travelling on the road.

VI. Whatever churches they are possessed of, no one is to deprive them of them.

VII. Whosoever shall annul any of these my decrees, let him know positively that he annuls the ordinance of God.

VIII. Moreover, neither their judges, governors, monks, servants, disciples, or any others depending on them, shall pay any poll tax, or be molested on that account, because I am their protector, wheresoever they shall be, either by land or sea, east or west, north or south; because both they and all that belong to them are included in this my promissory oath and patent.

IX. And of those that live quietly and solitary upon the mountains, they shall exact neither poll tax nor tithes from their incomes, neither shall any Mussulman partake of what they have, for they labour only to maintain themselves.

X. Whenever the crop of the earth shall be plentiful in its due time, the inhabitants shall be obliged, out of every bushel, to give them a certain measure.

XI. Neither in time of war shall they take them out of their habitation, nor compel them to go to the wars, nor even then shall they require of them any poll-tax.

In these eleven chapters is to be found whatever relates to the monks; as to the remaining seven chapters they direct what relates to every Christian.

XII. Those Christians who are inhabitants, and with their riches and traffic are able to pay the poll-tax, shall pay no more than 12 drachmas.

XIII. Excepting this, nothing more shall be required of them, according to the express word of God, that says:

"Do not molest those that have a veneration for the Books that are sent from God, but rather, in a kind manner, give of your good things to them, and converse with them, and hinder every one from molesting them."

XIV. If a Christian woman shall happen to marry a Mussulman, the Mussulman shall not cross the inclination of his wife to keep her from her chapel and prayers and the practice of her religion.*

XV. That no person hinder them from repairing their churches.

XVI. Whosoever acts contrary to this my grant, or gives credit to anything contrary to it, becomes truly an apostate from God and his divine Apostle, because this protection I have granted to them according to this promise.

XVII. No one shall bear arms against them, but, on the contrary, the Mussulmans shall wage war for them.

XVIII. And by this I ordain that none of my nation shall presume to do or act contrary to this promise until the end of the world.

Witnesses :

Ali, the Son of Abu Thaleb.
Homar, the son of Hattavi.
Ziphir, the son of Abuan.
Saith, the son of Maat
Thavitt, the son of Nesis.
Amphachin, the son of Hassan.
Muathem, the son of Kasvi.
Azur, the son of Jassin.
Abombaker, the son of Ambi Kaphe.
Ottman, the son of Gafas.
Ambtelack, the son of Messutt.

* Turkish lawyers give as an example of this point, that the Mussulman son of a Christian mother is bound to convey her, when old or infirm, to the church door, upon a beast (horse or mule, &c.) ; and should he be poor and possess no beast, he is bound to carry her on his shoulders.

Phazer, the son of Abbas.

Talat, the son of Amptonlack.

Saat, the son of Abbatt.

Kasmer, the son of Abid.

Ambtullack, the son of Omar.

This present was written by the leader, the successor of Ali, the son of Abu Thaleb ; the prophet marking it with his own hand at the Mosque of the Prophet (on whom be peace !) in the second year of the Hegira, the third day of the month, of Machorem." *

The above facts and arguments will, it is presumed, suffice to convince every candid and unprejudiced mind that this second charge against Mohammed being utterly devoid of foundation, is, therefore, both false and scandalous.

CHARGE III.

The sensual character of his Paradise as described by the Koran.

Another charge brought against Mohammed is the sensual character of the joys promised by him in his Paradise to those who shall receive his Law, and conform their lives to the precepts it contains ; but upon reflection, it will be found that there is nothing so absurd in this as is generally imagined by Christians, when it is considered that our bodies will, as we are told, assume, at the resurrection, a form so perfect as infinitely to surpass all that we can conceive, and that our senses will acquire so extraordinary an activity and vigour as to be susceptible of the greatest pleasures, each according to the difference of their objects, for,

* Mohammed himself had recommended the Christian sectaries to his captains, and had granted them protections which were confirmed by the third Caliph Omar, and preserved and continued under Othman and Ali.

It not being customary in those days to date documents, it is very probable that the original patent had no date, and that the one given in the text was assigned it at a subsequent period by the writer.

indeed, if we take away from those faculties their proper exercise, if we deprive them of the fit objects to please and gratify them it cannot be otherwise than supposed that they have not only been given us to no purpose, but even to inflict upon us continual disappointment and pain. For, in fact, by supposing that the soul and body are restored to us, as must necessarily be the case if our bodies are restored in a perfect state, it is not clear upon what grounds it can be supposed that the senses should not have objects to exercise upon, in order to be capable of bestowing, and of tasting all the pleasures which they may be capable of affording. Can there be any sin, crime, shame or degradation in the enjoyment of such pleasures? And as to that pleasure, more particularly denounced—that of the sexes—did not the Almighty institute and grant it to the two most perfect creatures who ever appeared in the world? and as the Almighty had freely and liberally provided for them, what-ever was necessary for the preservation of life, so He made them susceptible of the most rapturous delight in the act and duty of multiplying their species.

That Mohammed, in his Koran, promises the faithful the use of women, and mentions delightful gardens and other sensual delights, is true, but that he places the chief happi-ness in these things, is a mistake. For as the soul is more noble than the body, so he was willing to allow the body its own pleasures, that by the reward he promised he might the more easily allure the rude Arabians who thought of nothing but what was gross and sensual, to fall into the worship of the one and only true God, as expounded in his doctrine. But Mohammed always assigned to the soul its own peculiar pleasures, viz., the beholding the face of God, which will be the greatest of all delights, the fulness of joy, and which will cause all the other pleasures of Paradise to be forgotten, they being common to the cattle which graze in the field. He that beholdeth his gardens, wives, goods, and servants, reaching through the space of a thousand years' journey, is but in the lowest degree among the inhabitants of Paradise; but among them *he is in the supreme degree of honour with Gód, who contemplates His divine countenance every morn.* It is, therefore, false that the pleasures of the Mohammedan Paradise consist exclusively in corporeal things and the use of them; it is false, also, that all Mohammedans believe those pleasures to be corporeal, for many contend, on the contrary, that those things are said parabolically and are to be considered as of spiritual delights, in the same manner as the Doctors of the Christian Church maintain that "Solomon's Song" is not a mere Epithalamium, but is to be understood in a spiritual sense as typical of Christ's love for His Church.*

The famous Hyde, in his ' Not: ad Biboi, Turcar, Liturg.' p. 21, writes, " That those sensual pleasures of Paradise are thought by wiser Mohammedans to be allegorical—that they may be then better conceived by human understanding, just as in the Holy Scriptures many things are said after the manner of men. For writing to the Morocco ambassador, when I mentioned a garden pleasant, like that of Paradise, he, checking me, wrote back that Paradise was such a place to which nothing in the world could be likened; such as neither eye hath seen, ear heard, neither hath it entered into the heart of man to conceive." To this may likewise be added, the testimony of the famous Herbelot who, after having shewn in his ' Bibliotheca Orientalis,' that the Mohammedans place the chief good in the Communion of God, and the celestial joys in the fruition of the light of the Divine countenance which makes Paradise wherever it is, writes thus:—" It is not, therefore, true which many

* " A Moslem of some learning professed to me that he considered the description of Paradise (given in the Koran) to be, in a great measure, figurative, 'like those,' said he, 'in the book of the Revelations of St. John,' and he assured me that many learned Moslems were of the same opinion." (Lane's ' Modern Egypt,' vol. i. p. 75, note.)

authors who have opposed Mahometans, have asserted—
that the Mussulmans know no other happiness in Heaven
but the use of pleasures which affect the senses."

From what precedes, it follows that much more than is
just has been said and written about the sensual character
of Mohammed's religion. No doubt that from a Christian
point of view, and taken in the abstract, certain usages of
the peoples of the East present themselves to European
criticism as real defects and as great vices, but with a little
more of evangelical charity we should treat them less
severely. We should take more into account the influence
of origin and climate and the material necessity of social
obligations.

Equally mistaken, if not wilfully unjust, are those who
find in Mohhammed's sensual Paradise, a reflex of his own
character, and represent the Prophet (impostor they call
him) as a sensual voluptary, for so much to the contrary, he
was a poor, hard-toiling, ill-provided man, careless of what
vulgar men so eagerly labour and contend for.

CHARGE IV.

The encouragement Mohammed has given to licentiousness by
legalizing Polygamy.

Polygamy was a custom general throughout the East, so
long back as the days of the Patriarch Abraham, and which,
it is certain, from innumerable passages in Scripture, some
of which we shall quote, could not in those purer ages of
mankind, have been regarded as sinful.

Polygamy was permitted among the ancient Greeks, as
in the case of the detachment of young men from the army,
mentioned by Plutarch. It was also defended by Euripides
and Plato. The ancient Romans were more sévere in their
morals, and never practised it, although it was not forbidden
among them : and Marc Antony is mentioned as the first

who took the liberty of having two wives. From that time it became pretty frequent in the empire till the reigns of Theodosius, Honorius and Arcadius, who first prohibited it by an express law, A.D. 393. After this the Emperor Valentinian permitted, by an edict, all the subjects of the empire, if they pleased, to marry several wives; nor does it appear from the ecclesiastical history of those times, that the bishops made any objection to its introduction. Valentinianus Constantius, son of Constantine the Great, had many wives. Clotaire, King of France, and Heribartus and Hypericus his sons, had a plurality also. Add to these, Pepin and Charlemagne, of whom St. Urspergensus witnesses that they had several wives, Lothaire and his son, as likewise Arnolphus VII., Emperor of Germany (A.D. 888), and a descendant of Charlemagne, Frederic Barbarossa and Philip Theodatus King of France. Among the first race of the Kings of the Franks, Gontran, Caribert, Sigebert and Chilperic had several wives, at one time. Gontran had within his palace Veneranda and Mercatrude and Ostregilde, acknowledged as his legitimate wives; Caribert had Merflida, Marconesa and Theodogilda.

Father Daniel confesses the polygamy of the French Kings. He denies not the three wives of Dagobert I., expressly asserting that Theodobert espoused Dentary, although she had a husband, and himself, another wife, named Visigelde. He adds, that in this he imitated his uncle Clotaire, who espoused the widow of Creodomir, although he had already three wives.

With respect to the physiological reasons for polygamy, it has been observed by the celebrated Montesquieu that women in hot climates are marriageable at eight, nine or ten years of age; thus, in those countries, infancy and marriage almost always go together. They are old at twenty. Their reason, therefore, never accompanies their beauty. When beauty demands the empire the want of reason forbids the claim; when reason is obtained, beauty is no more. These women must necessarily be in a state of dependence; for reason cannot procure, in old age, that empire which even youth and beauty combined could not bestow. It is therefore extremely natural that in these places a man, when no law opposes it, should leave one wife to take another, and that polygamy should be introduced.

In temperate climates, where the charms of women are best preserved, where they arrive later at maturity and have children at a more advanced season of life, the old age of their husbands, in some degree, follows theirs: and as they have more reason and knowledge at the time of marriage, if it be only on account of their having continued longer in life, it must naturally introduce a kind of equality between the sexes, and, in consequence of this, the law of having only one wife. Nature, which has distinguished men by their reason and bodily strength, has set no other bounds to their power than those of this strength and reason. It has given charms to women, and ordained that their ascendancy over men shall end with those charms; but in hot countries these are found only at the beginning, and never in the progress of life.

Thus the law which permits only one wife is physically conformable to the climate of Europe, and not to that of Asia. This is the reason why Mohammedanism was established with such facility in Asia, and extended with so much difficulty in Europe; why Christianity is maintained in Europe, and has been destroyed in Asia; and, in fine, why the Mohammedans have made such progress in China and the Christians so little.

It appears, from Cæsar, that in early times our ancestors practised polyandry, ten or twelve husbands having only one wife among them.

When the Roman Catholic missionaries came among

these primitive people, they encouraged celibacy, and held that the marriage of a man with a widow was bigamy, and punishable canonically. At length we subsided into monogamy, as appears to have been the practice of the ancient Germans, agreeably to Tacitus ('De Moribus Germanorum.')*

As to the lawfulness of polygamy, it will be seen by referring to the following passages in Scripture that it was not only approved but even blessed by Jehovah himself:— Genesis, xxx., v. 22; Exodus, xxi., v. 11; Deuteronomy, xvii., v. 17; 1 Samuel, i., v. 1. 2, 11, 20; 1 Samuel, xxv., v. 42, 43; 2 Samuel, xii., v. 8; 2 Samuel, v., v. 13; Judges, viii., v. 30; Judges, x., v. 4: Judges, xii., v. 9, 14.

St. Chrysostom, speaking of Abraham and Hagar, says, "These things were not then forbidden." So St. Augustine observes that "there was a *blameless* custom of one man having many wives, which at that time might be done in a way of *duty*, which now cannot be done but from licentiousness, because, for the sake of multiplying posterity, *no law forbad a plurality of wives.*†

Boniface, Confessor of Lower Germany, having consulted Pope Gregory, in the year 726, in order to know in what cases a husband might be allowed to have two wives, Gregory replied, on the 22nd November of the same year, in these words—"If a wife be attacked by a malady which renders her unfit for conjugal intercourse, the husband may marry another, but in that case he must allow his sick wife all necessary support and assistance."

Many works have been published in defence of polygamy even by writers professing Christianity. Bernardo Ochinus, General of the Order of Capuchins, published, about the middle of the sixteenth century, dialogues in favour of the practice, and about the same time appeared a treatise on

* Prope soli barbarorum singulis uxoribus contenti sunt.
† See Grotius, 'De Jure,' vol. i. p. 268, note.

behalf of a plurality of wives ; the author, whose real name was Lysarus, having assumed the pseudo one of Theophilus Aleuthes.

Selden proves, in his ' Uxor Hebraica,' that polygamy was allowed not only among the Jews, but likewise among all other nations.

But the most distinguished defender of polygamy was the celebrated John Milton, who, in his ' Treatise on Christian Doctrine,* after quoting various passages from the Bible in defence of the practice, says, " Moreover, God, in an allegorical fiction (Ezekiel, xxiii.), represents Himself as having espoused two wives, Aholah and Aholiah,—a mode of speaking which Jehovah would by no means have employed, especially at such length even in a parable, nor, indeed, have taken upon himself such a character at all, if the practice which it implied had been intrinsically dishonourable or shameful."

" On what grounds, then, can a practice be considered as so dishonourable or shameful which is prohibited to no one even under the Gospel ; for that dispensation annuls none of the merely civil regulations which existed previously to its introduction.   It is only enjoined that elders and deacons should be chosen from such as were husbands of one wife (1. Tim., iii., v. 2, and Tim., i., 6).   This implies, not that to be the husband of more than one wife would be a sin, for, in that case, the restriction would have been equally imposed on all, but that in proportion as they were less entangled in domestic affairs, they would be more at leisure for the business of the Church.   Since, therefore, polygamy is interdicted in this passage to the ministers of the Church alone, and that, not on account of any sinfulness in the practice, and since none of the other members are precluded from it, either here or elsewhere, it follows that it was permitted, as aforesaid, to all the remaining members of

* Page 237 et seq.

the Church, and that it was adopted by many without offence."

"Lastly, I argue as follows, from Hebrews, xiii. v. 4 :— Polygamy is either marriage, fornication or adultery. The Apostle recognises no fourth state. Reverence for so many patriarchs who were polygamists will, I trust, deter every one from considering it as fornication or adultery, for '*whoremongers and adulterers God will judge*,' whereas the Patriarchs were the objects of his especial favour, as he himself witnesses. If, then, polygamy be marriage properly so called, it is also lawful and honourable : according to the same Apostle, '*marriage is honourable in all and the bed undefiled*.'"

Mohammed, therefore, did but legalize a practice not only honoured but even blessed by God himself, under the old dispensation, and declared to be lawful and honourable under the new one ; and, consequently, he must be exonerated from the charge of having sanctioned polygamy, and thereby encouraged licentiousness.

The chief arguments adduced against polygamy are that it introduces into the matrimonial state a despotic usurpation which destroys the equality of rank between the sexes ; that it is destructive of real love and friendship ; that it is the parent of jealousy and domestic dissensions.

The belief that the possessor of a harem of wives in those countries where polygamy is permitted, exercises a despotic sway over them, is one of those errors which Western people adopt from their ignorance of Asiatic manners. Where marital discipline prevails in the East it is on the contrary, amongst those whom poverty condemns to monogamy. It often happens that where there are many wives, one will rule the rest, and the husband into the bargain. Those who have looked into the works written by natives of the East, which give true particulars of Oriental manners, will at once perceive that the notion of women being the objects of domestic tyranny in that part of the world is merely ideal. "Little," says Mr. Atkinson,* "is understood in England of the real situation of women in the East beyond the impression of their being everywhere absolute slaves to their tyrant husbands, and cooped up in a harem, which to them, it is supposed, can be nothing better than a prison." But this he denies, and he shows how much power and how many privileges Mohammedan women possess. So far from the harem being a prison to the wives, it is a place of liberty, where the husband himself is treated as an interloper. The moment his foot passes the threshold, everything reminds him that he is no lónger lord and master; children, servants and slaves look alone to the principal lady; in short, she is paramount : when she is in good humour, everything goes on well, and when in bad, nothing goes right. Mirza Abu Thaleb Khan, a Persian nobleman who visited England between sixty and eighty years ago, and paid great attention to our domestic habits, in the account of his visit which he afterwards published, and which was translated into English, assigns reasons to show that the Mohammedan women have more power and liberty, and are invested with greater privileges than European ones, and he annihilates at once the notion of the marital despotism of polygamy, by observing, "From what I know it is easier to live with two tigresses than with two wives."

The celebrated traveller Niebuhr is of the same opinion.— "Europeans," he observes,† "are mistaken in thinking that the state of marriage is so different amongst the Mohammedans from what it is with Christian nations. I could not discern any such difference in Arabia. The women of that country seem to be as free and happy as those of Europe can possibly be. Polygamy is permitted, indeed, amongst

---

* ' Customs and Manners of the Women of Persia.'
† ' Travels.'·

Mohammedans, and the delicacy of our ladies is shocked at this idea; but the Arabians rarely avail themselves of the privileges of marrying four lawful wives, and entertaining, at the same time, any number of female slaves. None but rich voluptuaries marry so many wives, and their conduct is blamed by all sober men. Men of sense, indeed, think the privilege rather troublesome than convenient. A husband is, by law, obliged to treat his wives suitably to their condition, and to dispense his favours amongst them with perfect equality! but these are duties not a little disagreeable to most Mussulmans, and such modes of luxury are too expensive to the Arabians, who are seldom in easy circumstances."

Then as to its being destructive of real love and friendship, it may be doubted whether among the higher classes in this hemisphere, to whom polygamy, if permitted, would be chiefly confined (owing to the expense it would entail in establishments), there would be less real and less reciprocal friendship in a second or third connection than at present in the first. The cold formality of marriage settlements, pin-money, the separate carriages, and other domestic arrangements common among the upper classes, must destroy all the tender sentiments which belong to pure, disinterested love; and women in our fashionable life are more frequently bought and sold than in polygamic countries.

As to polygamy being an extinguisher of love, this is a notion springing from the same source of absurd prejudices as that which suggests Old England to be the only land of liberty and happiness. If polygamy deserved all the hard things said of it, if it was the source of so many evils and the spring of so few enjoyments, we should scarcely see it in vogue throughout so large a portion of the world, where refinement has made so little progress.

M

PART IV.

BEAUTIES OF THE KORAN.

BEAUTIES OF THE KORAN.

SOLE CHAPTER.

Alms-giving, its reward—Happiness of true believers in Paradise—Creation of the world—God, no God but the One who is without peers and eternal—All His works praise Him—Refutation of the assertion that Jehovah rested from His labours on the seventh day—*Corsi*, God's throne or tribunal (note)—God's universal presence—It beseemeth not God to beget children—Path of happiness or of misery, for whom—Ingratitute of man towards God—Terrors of the Day of Judgment; the atom's weight of good and the atom's weight of evil—Under what circumstances the soul shall be made to know the sins it has committed—Accountability of irrational animals—Infanticide—Kindness and respect due to parents, Al Forkan (note)—The Koran not to be touched but by the purified (note)—Just balance—The Koran a mission from God to Mohammed—God's protection of Mohammed—Wine and games of chance forbidden—Respect and love for parents (note)—Justice towards orphans—True piety—Prayer enjoined - Punishment of the slanderer—The soul, how preserved and how lost—Women.

Alms.

Whatsoever ye put out at usury, to increase with the substance of others, shall have no increase from God; but whatsoever ye shall give in alms, as seeking the face of God, shall be doubled unto you.

Fear God, then, with all your might, and hear and obey, and give alms for your own weal; for such as are saved from their own greed, shall prosper.

They who give away their substance in alms, by night and day, in private and public, shall have their reward with their Lord; no fear shall come upon them, neither shall they be put to grief.

And whatsoever ye shall give, and whatsoever ye shall vow, of a truth, God knoweth it, but they who act unjustly shall have no helpers. Give ye your alms openly? it is well. Do ye conceal them and give them to the poor? this, too, is well, and will advantage you and will cleanse you of your sins. God is cognizant of your actions.

BELIEVERS (THE REWARD OF).

But to those who have believed and done the things which are right (we will lay on no one a burden beyond his power to bear) these shall be inmates of Paradise, for ever shall they abide therein.

And we will remove whatever rancour was in their bosoms; rivers shall flow at their feet, and they shall say, "Praise be to God, who hath guided us hither! We had not been guided, had not God guided us! Of a surety the apostles of our Lord came to us with truth," and a voice shall say unto them, "This is Paradise, of which as the meed of your works, ye are made heirs."

But for those who have believed and done the things that are right, we will bring them into gardens 'neath which the rivers flow—therein to abide eternally; therein shall they have wives of stainless purity; and them will we bring into aye-shadowing glades.

CREATION.

It is GOD who hath created the heavens without pillars thou canst behold; then ascended He His throne, and to the sun and moon assigned he laws, each travelleth to its appointed goal. He ordereth all things. He maketh his signs clear that ye may have firm faith in a meeting with your Lord.

He (God) hath created the heavens and the earth to set forth his truth; high let Him be exalted above the gods they join with Him.

Do ye, indeed, disbelieve in Him who, in two days, created the earth? and do ye assign unto Him peers? The Lord of the Worlds is He.

And He hath placed on the earth the firm mountains which above it tower; and He hath blessed it and distributed food throughout for the cravings of all alike, in four days.

Then applied He himself unto the heaven which then was but smoke, and to it and the earth did He say: "Come ye, whether in obedience or against your will;" and they both replied: "We come, obedient."

God!—there is no God but He, the Living, the Eternal! Nor slumber seizeth Him, nor sleep. His, whatsoever is in the heavens and whatsoever is in the earth. Who is there that can intercede with Him but by His own permission? He knoweth what hath been before them (the heavens and the earth), and what shall be after them, yet nought of His knowledge shall they comprehend, save that which He willeth. His throne is extended high over heaven and earth, and the upholding of both is no burden to Him;— He is the High—the Mighty! *

Whatsoever is in heaven and earth singeth praise unto God. He is mighty and wise. His is the kingdom of heaven and earth. He giveth life and He putteth to death, and He is almighty. He is the first and the last; the

---

* This throne, in Arabic called *Corsi*, is by the Mohammedans supposed to be God's tribunal, or seat of justice; being placed under the other, which is called *AlArjsh*, being His imperial throne. The *Corsi*, allegorically, signifies—the divine providence, which sustains and governs the heaven and the earth, and is infinitely above all human comprehension.

manifest and the hidden; and He knoweth all things;—it is He who created the heavens and the earth in six days, and then ascended the throne.*   He knoweth that which entereth the earth and that which issueth out of the same, and that which descendeth from heaven and that which ascendeth thereto; and He is with you, wheresoever ye may be; for God seeth that which ye do.   His is the kingdom of heaven and earth, and unto God do all things return.   He causeth the night to succeed the day, and He causeth the day to succeed the night; and He knoweth the innermost parts of men's hearts.

GOD.†

Praise be unto God, the Lord of creation,
The all-merciful, the all-compassionate!
        Ruler of the Day of Reckoning!
Thee do we worship, and Thee do we invoke for help.
        Lead us in the straight path,
The path of those to whom Thou hast been gracious,
Not in that of those who are the objects of wrath,
        Or who walk in error!

        Say: " He is God alone;
        God! the Eternal!
        He begetteth not and is not begotten,
        Nor is there any like unto Him."

---

* " We created the heavens and the earth, and whatever is between them in six days; and no weariness affected us" (Koran, chap. 50).   Upon this passage Sale observes, " This was revealed in answer to the Jews, who said that God rested from his work of creation on the seventh day, and reposed himself on his throne as one fatigued."

† This prayer is recited several times in each of the five daily prayers, as well as on many other occasions, as in concluding a bargain, entering into an engagement, etc.   It is called ' The Initial Prayer,' and answers to the ' Lord's Prayer' of the Christians.   The Mohammedans hold it in the utmost reverence, giving it several other honourable titles, as the chapter of *prayer*, of *praise*, of *thanksgiving*, of *treasure*, etc., and esteeming it as the quintessence of the Koran.

Blessed be He in whose hands is the kingdom, and over
      All things is He potent.
Who hath created Death and Life, to prove which
      Of you is most righteous in his deeds.
He is the mighty—the forgiving,
Who hath created seven heavens, one above another;
No defect can'st thou discover in the creation of
The God of Mercy : repeat thy gaze, and it
      Shall return unto thee dulled and weary.

Perceivest thou not that God knoweth whatever is in heaven and in earth ?   There is no private discourse among three persons, but He is the fourth of them ; nor among five, but he is the sixth of them ; neither among a smaller number than this, nor a larger, but He is with them, wheresoever they may be ; and He will declare unto them that which they have done, on the day of resurrection, for God knoweth all things.

With God are the keys of the secret things ;
      None knoweth them besides Himself ;
He knoweth that which is on the dry land, and in the sea ;
      There falleth not a leaf but He knoweth it ;
Neither is there a single grain in the dark recesses of the
      earth,
      Neither a green thing, nor a dry thing,
But it is written in the perspicuous Book.

Glory unto Him (God)! immensely high is He exalted !
The seven heavens praise Him, the earth and all who are
      therein.
      Neither is there aught which doth not celebrate His power ;
      But their utterance of praise ye understand not.

With Him (God) are the secrets of the heavens and the earth.
      Look thou and hearken unto Him alone !

Man hath no guardian but He, nor many share in his
    judgments.

Whatever is in the heaven and the earth—is God's ;
    And whether you bring forth to light what is in your minds,
        Or conceal the same,
God will surely reckon with you for it.

Swear not by God, when ye make oath that ye will be
virtuous and fear God, and promote peace among men ; for
God is He who Heareth, Knoweth.

God will not punish you for a mistake in your oaths ;
but He will punish you for that which your hearts have
done. God is Gracious, Merciful.

To God belong the secret things of the heavens and the earth;
    Unto Him all things return ;
Worship Him then and put your trust in Him ;
Thy Lord is not regardless of thy doings.

Oh men ! ye are paupers in need of God, but God is the
rich, the praiseworthy.

Who supplieth you from heaven and earth ? Who hath
power over hearing and sight ? and who bringeth forth the
living from the dead, and the dead from the living ? Surely,
they will answer—" God !" then say : " What, will ye not
therefore fear Him ?"

Doth any one desire greatness ? All greatness is in God.
The good word riseth up to Him, and the righteous deed
will He exalt. But a terrible punishment awaiteth the
planner of iniquity, and the machinations of such will He
surely confound.

They say, the Merciful hath begotten issue. Now have
ye uttered an impious thing ; it wanteth little but on occa-

sion thereof, the heavens be rent, and the earth cleave asunder, and the mountains fall down in fragments, for that they attribute a son to the God of mercy, when it beseemeth not the All-merciful to beget children. Verily, there is none in heaven and in earth but shall approach the Merciful as His servant.

HAPPINESS AND MISERY (FOR WHOM).

By the NIGHT when she spreadeth her veil ;
By the DAY when she brightly shineth ;
By HIM who created the male and female ;
Of a truth, at different ends do ye aim !
But as for him who giveth alms and feareth God,
And yieldeth assent unto the good :
Unto him will We make easy the path to happiness ;
But as for him who is covetous and bent upon riches,
And who calleth the Good, a lie,
Unto him will We make easy the path of misery.

It is God who hath given you the earth as a sure foundation. and over it built the heavens and formed you and made your form comely, and feedeth you with good things. This is God your Lord. Blessed then be God, the Lord of the Worlds ! He is the living God. No god is there, except He. Call, therefore, upon Him and offer unto Him a pure worship. Praise be unto God, the Lord of the Worlds ! It is He who giveth life and death ; and when He decreeth a thing, He only saith of it : "Be," and it is.

INGRATITUDE (OF MAN TO GOD).

By the snorting chargers !
And the war-horses that dash off sparks of fire !
And those that rush to the attack at morn !
And stir therein the dust aloft !

And cleave therein their midway through a host !
Truly man to his Lord ungrateful is,
And of this he is himself a witness :
And truly he is keen in the love of this world's good ;
Ah ! wotteth he not that when that which is in the grave
            Shall be laid bare,
And that which is in men's hearts shall be brought forth ?
Verily, their Lord shall, on that day, be informed
            Concerning them.

JUDGMENT DAY.

On that day (the last) there shall be a blast upon the
trumpet, and all that are on earth shall be terror-stricken,
save him whom God pleaseth to deliver ; and all shall come
unto him as suppliants.

And thou shalt see the mountains, which thou thinkest
so firm, dissolve away like unto the passing of a cloud.
'Tis the work of God, who ordereth all things.   Of all that
ye do, He is well aware.

When the Earth with her quaking shall tremble,
And the Earth shall cast forth her burdens.
And men shall cry, " What aileth her ? "
On that day shall she unfold her tidings,
For, verily, the Lord shall have inspired her.
On that day shall the sons of men come forward in ranks.
            To behold their works ;
And whosoever an atom's weight of good shall have wrought
            Shall behold the same ;
And whosoever an atom's weight of evil shall have wrought
            Shall behold the same.

When the heavens shall cleave asunder,
And when the stars shall be scattered,
And when the oceans shall be commingled,

And when the graves shall be turned upside down,
Each soul shall behold its earliest and its latest deeds.

But when one blast shall be blown on the trumpet,
And the earth and the mountains shall be upheaved,
And shall both be crushed into dust at a single crushing,
On that day the woe that must come suddenly shall
Suddenly come,
And the heaven shall cleave asunder, for on that day
it shall be fragile :
On that day ye shall be brought before Him ;
Nor shall any of your hidden deeds remain concealed.

When the sun shall be FOLDED UP,*
And when the stars shall fall,
And when the mountains shall be made to pass away,
And when the camels ten months gone with young, shall be
neglected,†
And when the wild beasts shall be gathered together,‡
And when the seas shall boil,
And when souls shall be again united to their bodies,
And when the female child that had been buried alive shall
be asked
For what crime she was put to death,§
And when the leaves of the Book shall be laid open,
And when the Heaven shall be stripped away,‖
And when Hell thall be made to blaze,

* That is, like a garment that is laid by.

† To express the greatness of the terror of the day, the she-camels with young (a most valuable part of the substance of Arabs) shall be utterly neglected.

‡ For the Mohammedans believe that not only mankind, but irrational animals also, shall be judged on that tremendous day ; when the unarmed cattle shall take vengeance on the horned, till entire satisfaction shall be given to the injured.

§ For it was customary among the ancient Arabs to bury their daughters alive, as soon as born, for fear they should become impoverished by providing for them, or should suffer disgrace on their account.

‖ Like a skin from an animal when flayed.

And when Paradise shall be brought near,
THEN shall every soul know what it hath wrought.

KINDNESS AND HOSPITALITY (RECOMMENDED).

Be good unto parents,* and to kindred, and to orphans, and to the poor, and to a neighbour, whether kinsman or new-comer, and to a fellow-traveller, and to the wayfarer, and to the slaves which your right hands hold.

Moreover, we have enjoined on man to show kindness unto his parents. With pain his mother beareth him; with pain she bringeth him forth; and his bearing and weaning are thirty months, and when he attaineth his strength and attaineth to forty years, he saith, " O, Lord! cause me to be grateful for thy favours wherewith thou hast favoured me and my parents.

KORAN (THE).

BLESSED be He who hath sent down AL FORKAN† (the illu-
    minator) unto his servant, that unto all creatures he
    may be a warner.
His the kingdom of the Heavens and of the Earth!
No son hath He begotten! No partner hath He in His
    empire!
All things hath He created,
    And, decreeing, hath decreed their destinies!

By the STAR when it setteth,
Your companion Mohammed erreth not, nor is he led astray;

---

* An undutiful son is very seldom heard of among the Egyptians or the Arabians, in general. Sons scarcely ever sit, or eat, or smoke, in the presence of the father, unless bidden to do so; and they often wait upon him and upon his guests at meals, and on other occasions; they do not cease to act thus when they become men." (Lane's 'Modern Egypt,' vol. i.)

† The word *Forkan*, taken in a general sense, means *illumination, deliverance*; it was derived by Mohammed from the Jews, who applied it to the Pentateuch in the same manner as the Arabian prophet applied it to the Koran.

Neither doth he speak of his own will.
The KORAN is no other than a Revelation revealed to him ;
One mighty in power* endued with wisdom taught it him.

What think ye ? the fire which ye strike,
Do ye produce the tree whence ye obtain the same,
Or are We the producers thereof ?
We have ordained the same for an admonition,†
And an advantage to the wayfarers of the desert.
Wherefore praise the name of thy Lord, the great GOD.
Moreover, I swear by the setting of the stars,
(And it is a great oath, if ye knew it)
That this is the honourable KORAN,
The original of which is written in the preserved Book :‡
Let none touch it but the purified ;§
It is a revelation from the Lord of all creatures.

MEASURE (SHOULD BE JUST).

Woe unto those who STINT the measure or weight !
Who when they take by measure from others exact the full,
But when they mete out or weigh to them minish !
What, have they no thought that they shall be raised again ?
For the Great Day, that Day when mankind
Shall stand before the Lord of the Worlds ?

The Lord of mercy hath taught his servant the KORAN,
Hath created man, and taught him articulate speech.
The sun and the moon have each their times,
And the plants and the trees bend in adoration.

---

* The angel Gabriel, to the meaning of whose name, as the *strong one of God*, these words probably apply.

† To put men in mind of the resurrection, which the production of fire in some sort resembles, or of the fire of hell.

‡ That is, the prototype of the Koran written down in the book kept by God himself. (See p. 64.)

§ Purity both of mind and body being requisite in him who should use this book with the respect he ought, and hopes to edify by it ; for which reason these words are usually written on the cover. (See p. 69.)

And the Heaven hath He reared it up on high,
        And hath appointed a balance;
That in the balance ye should not transgress;
Weigh, therefore, with fairness, and scant not the balance.

The STRIKING !* what is the striking ?
Who shall teach thee what the striking is ?
The day when men shall be like scattered moths,
And the mountains shall be like flocks of carded wool.
Then as to him whose balances are heavy—his
        Shall be a life that shall please Him well;
As to him whose balances are light, his
        Dwelling-place shall be the pit.
And who shall make thee to understand
        How frightful the pit (of Hell) is !
        Verily is it a raging fire !

MOHAMMED.

(The Koran sent down to him.)

Not to sadden thee (Mohammed) have We sent down
        This KORAN unto thee,
        But as a warning for whomsoever feareth;
        It is a missive from Him
Who hath made the Earth and the lofty Heavens.
The God of mercy sitteth on His throne.
        His whatsoever is in the Heavens,
        And whatsoever is on the Earth,
        And whatsoever is between them both,
And whatsoever is beneath the humid soil;
        No need hast thou to raise thy voice, for
He knoweth the secret whisper, and what is yet more hidden.

---

* Sometimes called " The *Blow*." This is one of the names or epithets given to the last day, because it will *strike* the hearts of all creatures with terror.

God! there is no God but He!
Most excellent are His titles.*
By the noonday brightness,†
And by the night when it darkeneth.
The Lord hath not forsaken thee,
Neither hath He been displeased.
Be assured the future shall be better for thee than the past,
And the Lord shall give thee a reward wherewith thou
 shalt be content;
Did He not find thee an orphan‡ and give thee a home?
And found thee erring, and guided thee?§
And found thee needy, and enriched thee?
Wherefore, oppress not the orphan, nor repulse the beggar,
 But declare the goodness of thy Lord.

Recite, thou, in the name of the Lord, who created—||
Created Man from nought but congealed blood.
Recite! for thy Lord is beneficent.
It is He who hath taught (to record Revelation) with a pen;
 Hath taught man what he knoweth not.

I swear by the declining day,¶
Verily, man's lot is cast amid destruction!
Save those who believe and do the things which are right,
And enjoin truth, and recommend stedfastness to one
 another.

* Expressing his glorious attributes. Of these the Mohammedan Arabs
have no less than ninety-three, which are reckoned up by Maracci in his
Al Coran, p. 414.

† This chapter is said to have been the expression of deep mental anxiety
into which Mohammed had fallen on account of not having been favoured
with any revelation for several days.

‡ The charge of Mohammed, when left an orphan, was undertaken by his
grandfather. (See p. 8.)

§ Up to his fortieth year, Mohammed had followed the religion of his
countrymen.

|| The command delivered by the angel Gabriel to Mohammed. (See
p. 15.)

¶ Said to have been recited in the Mosque shortly before his death, by
Mohammed.

N

MORAL INJUNCTIONS.

Have nought to do with adultery, for it is a foul thing and an evil way.

Speak unto the believers that they restrain their eyes and observe continence. Thus will they be more pure. God is well aware of what they do.

Walk not proudly on the earth, for thou canst not cleave the earth, neither canst thou equal the mountains in stature. All this is evil and abominable in the sight of the Lord.

Be patient with those who call upon the Lord at morn and even, seeking His face: and let not thine eyes be turned away from them in quest of the pomp of this life; neither obey him whose heart we have caused to neglect the remembrance of Us, and who followeth his lusts and leaveth the truth behind him.

Come, I will rehearse what your Lord hath made binding upon you: that ye assign not aught to Him as partner; that ye be good to your parents, and that ye slay not your children, because of poverty; for them and for you will We provide; that ye come not near to pollution, outward or inward, and that ye slay not one whom God hath forbidden you, unless for a just cause. This hath He enjoined on you, to the intent that ye may understand.

O believers! surely wine and games of chance,* and statues and the divining arrows† are an abomination of

---

* The strict observers of the letter of the Koran forbid even the game of chess, but the Persians and Indians are generally more liberal in their interpretation of this verse.

† For the mode of casting lots by arrows, much practised among the Pagan Arabs, see Sale's 'Preliminary Discourse,' sect. 5.

Satan's work! Avoid them, that ye may prosper. Satan seeketh to sow hatred and strife among you, by wine and games of chance, and to turn you aside from the remembrance of God and prayer; will ye not, therefore, abstain from them? Obey God, and obey the Apostle, and be upon your guard.

O, ye, who believe! stand fast to justice when ye bear witness before God, though it be against yourselves or your parents, or your kindred, whether the party be rich or whether he be poor. God is more worthy than both; therefore follow not your own lusts in bearing testimony, lest ye swerve from truth : and if ye wrest your testimony or decline giving it, God verily is aware of what ye do.

What thing is weightiest in bearing testimony? Say " God is witness between me and thee," and this Koran hath been revealed unto me that I should warn thereby both thee and all whom it may reach.

ORPHANS.

Give unto orphans their property ; substitute not worthless things of your own for their valuable ones; and devour not their substance, for this is a great sin.

And they will also enquire of thee concerning orphans. Say, " Fair dealing with them is best. But if ye intermeddle with the management of what belongs to them, do them no wrong, for they are your brethren : God knoweth the corrupt dealer from the righteous one; and if God please, He will surely distress you.*

PARENTS.

The Lord hath ordained that ye worship none but Him,

---

* By his curse, which will certainly bring to nothing what the orphans shall have been robbed of.

and that ye show kindness to your parents, whether one ⌐
both of them attain to old age with thee; and say not to them
" Fie !" neither reproach them, but with respectful speech
address them both, deferring humbly to them out of tenderness; and say, " Lord have compassion on them both, even
as they reared me when I was a little one !"

Moreover We have enjoined on man to show kindness
unto his parents. With pain his mother beareth him; with
pain she bringeth him forth; and his bearing and his
weaning are thirty months.*

PIETY.

There is no piety in turning your faces towards the East
or towards the West; but he is pious who believeth in God,
and the last day, and the angels, and the Scriptures; who,
for the love of God, disburseth his wealth to his kindred
and to the orphans and the needy and the wayfarer, and to
those who ask and for ransoms, who observeth prayer and
payeth the legal alms, and who is of those who are faithful
to their engagements when they have engaged in them, and
who are patient under hardships and in times of adversity;
these are they who are just and pious, these are they who
fear the Lord.

PRAYER.

Recite that which hath been revealed unto thee of the
Koran, and be constant in prayer, for prayer restraineth

* " An equally beautiful feature in the character of the Turks is their
reverence and respect for the author of their being. Their wives advise and
reprimand, unheeded, their words are—*bosh*, nothing ; but the mother is an
oracle. She is consulted, confided in, listened to with respect and deference,
honoured to her latest hour, and remembered with regret and affection
beyond the grave. 'My wives die, and I can replace them,' says the
Osmanli ; 'my children perish, and others may be born to me ; but who
shall restore to me the mother who has passed away, and who is seen no
more." (' City of the Sultan,' by Miss Pardoe, 4th edit. p. 36,)

from the filthy and the blame-worthy, and surely is the remembering of God a most important duty.

Be ye constant in prayer, and give alms ; and whatsoever good ye have done and sent before for your souls, ye shall find it with God; for, of a surety, God seeth that which ye do.

To God belongeth both the East and the West, therefore, whithersoever you turn yourselves to pray, there is God : for He is the Omnipresent, the Omniscient.

Verily, they who recite the Book of God, and observe prayer, and give alms in public and in private from what we have bestowed upon them, may hope for a merchandise that shall not perish.

SLANDERERS—BACKBITERS.

Woe to every slanderer and backbiter !
Who amasseth wealth, and storeth it against the future !
He thinketh surely that his wealth shall abide with him for
    ever.
Nay; for verily he shall be flung into the crushing Al
    Hotoma ; *
And who shall teach thee what that crushing Hotoma is ?
It is God's kindled fire,
Which shall mount above the hearts of the damned ;
It shall verily rise over them like unto an arched vault,
On columns of vast extent.

SOUL (THE).

By the sun and his noon-day brightness !
By the moon when she followeth him !
By the day when it revealeth His glory !

* One of the names of hell.

By the night when it enshroudeth him !
By the heaven, and by Him who built it !
By the earth, and by Him who spread it forth.
By the soul and Him who deftly fashioned it,
Endowing it with knowledge to distinguish
And power to choose, or righteousness, or iniquity ;
BLESSED is he who hath preserved HIS pure,
And LOST is he who hath defiled it !

WOMEN.

And speak to the believing women, that they refrain their eyes and observe continence; and that they display not their ornaments * except to their husbands or their fathers, or their sons or their husband's sons, or their women, or their slaves, or male domestics who have no natural power ; or to children who note not women's nakedness. And let them not strike their feet together, so as to discover their hidden ornaments.†

Neither let women laugh to scorn other women, who, haply, may be better than themselves. Neither defame one another, nor call one another by opprobrious names.

  * As their clothes, jewels, and the furniture of their toilet, much less such parts of their bodies as ought not to be seen.

  † The pride which the Jewish ladies of old, also, took in making a tinkling noise with the ornaments of their feet, such as rings, anklets, &c., which were usually of gold and silver, is severely reproved by the prophet Isaiah, iii. 16, 18.

THE END.

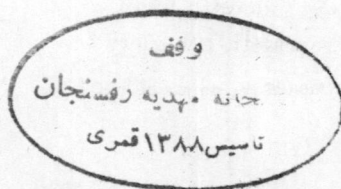